DUNAMIS

Daniel Confusione

Dunamis

ISBN-13: 978-1976517167
ISBN-10: 1976517168

Editing by
Mike Valentino
EditorMikeV@aol.com

Cover Image
SelfPubBookCovers.com/ RLSather

Printed and bound in USA
First Printing December 2017

Published by Booski Publishing
Contact@booskipublishing.com

O taste and see that the Lord is good: blessed is the man that trusteth in Him

Psalm 34:8

௵ DEDICATION ௵

This book is dedicated to Pastor Sylvester and Frances Confusione. Two people who have, without compromise, lived to the best of their abilities in sacrifice and obedience to the Lord's purpose in their lives. Always giving of themselves and everything they've had, even when that was very little. These two people have a dedication to Christ unlike anything I've seen. An uncompromising respect and love for the word of God which seems a seldom occurrence these days. Their hearts are like a mirror image of Christ's love, reflecting through them God's heart for others and through this love, they have been able to bring healing to countless people. Here are two people who continually look beyond themselves and their tribulations, always finding time to share God's love with others in need.

This book is not only a book of God's power and profound goodness in the lives of its characters, but it is just a small glimpse into the testimony that is Sylvester and Frances' life. With Jesus Christ at the center of their lives, they have touched countless souls. A humble Ministry, Loaves and Fishes Ministries, Inc., born out of anguish, started with serving simple sandwiches to the migrant workers on Long Island, NY. Little did they know this would be the beginning of a small ministry which would ultimately span the world. Israel, Uganda, Nigeria, India, Kenya, Malaysia, Mexico and Haiti are just some of the many countries that God's love was able to reach through their love and obedience to Christ. Only heaven knows the extent to which these two extraordinary people have been able to positively reach others, but if the fruit of their lives is any indication that number continues to grow to this day.

True devotion to their Lord and Savior Jesus Christ and a genuine love for others has kept Sylvester and Frances committed to praying, every morning, for everyone they know by name. For over three decades that list has grown extremely large but not a day goes by where one person is lost from their prayers. It is their genuine heart's desire that God's perfect will be exemplified in everyone's life and that they truly can experience what it means to be a child of the living Savior.

Sylvester and Frances knew early on that their purpose in life was to love people and through this love, hearts would be changed and uplifted. They've opened their home to those in need. They have given their own clothing, they've provided food when they had barely enough to feed themselves and because of this, despite extreme adversity and betrayal, through their own testimony, God has never left them wanting. They have never awaited a Nobel Prize, ceremony, or any special recognition. But, it was never about that. Sylvester and Frances have lived their lives with the purpose of serving their Lord and Savior, Jesus Christ. A small ministry started by two humble people with help from faithful hearts, such as those found in Nikola and Lorraine Baricevic, was able to reach across the world and show many just how amazing God's love is.

This book is dedicated to two special people who have passed on the most invaluable heirloom to not only family, but everyone with whom they've come into contact. An inheritance which speaks of the love and faithfulness of our Lord and Savior, Jesus Christ.

This book is dedicated to,

Pastor Sonny & Fran Confusione

Dad and Mom

Nikola & Lorraine Baricevic

How can I not regard them a blessing amongst those most cherished? A friendship inspired by God before the world's foundation was fashioned. Here are two special people, whose hearts have been faithfully knit alongside Pastor Sonny and Fran Confusione since God told them to step out in faith. Together they have pushed ahead under the banner of their Savior Jesus Christ, and have shared in witnessing the Lord's power on countless occasions. Together, they were called to spread God's love to the world and equally they share in the inheritance bestowed upon them by Christ their Savior. Nikola and Lorraine are the epitome of the Bible's definition of love, ever faithful hearts whose friendship is acknowledged for the perfect gift it is, one given by the Lord Christ Himself.

Robert & Barbara Seeley

We thank the Lord every day for considering us worthy enough to receive the blessing of such a friendship given in Bob and Barbara. Two extraordinary people who have continually demonstrated a love and faithfulness that far exceeds what words can describe. They are kindred hearts who have devotedly given of themselves fully to the purpose of Christ and have been able to be that loving foundation that others can look to. They've been used of the Lord to kindle countless souls and, through their steadfast devotion, have seen those sparks burst into a passionate desire for Christ. Thank you, Bob and Barbara for countless years of devoted friendship. It is our hearts' prayer that the Lord open the windows of heaven and bless you beyond your greatest expectations.

Pastor Charles & Colleen Silano

Pastor Charles and Colleen Silano are two wonderful people who have continued to share God's most amazing gift with others. That gift being 'the free and unmerited favor of the Lord'. Here are two people, filled with the Holy Spirit, whose hearts are solely dedicated to seeing God's fulfilled purpose in others. Through these humble hearts many have been able to find their healing, hope, and now peacefully reside inside the loving embrace of their Heavenly Father. Pastor Charles and Colleen Silano, thank you for your love and devotion to our Lord and Savior Jesus Christ and in turn for others. May you be exceedingly blessed for the love you have shown and continue to impart upon our family. You may never know just what an incredible blessing you truly are.

Pastor Michael Bryant

Pastor Michael Bryant is a devoted man of God set apart for such a time as this. A person who has been fashioned in the love and faithfulness of our Lord Jesus Christ, and through these characteristics, has been able to share hope and love with others. God has placed a special anointing on Pastor Bryant's life, which is clearly evident from the moment you meet him. What a blessing it is to see him, devotedly take up the mantle of Christ and run the race set before him, spreading words of hope, faith and love.

Before the very first words of this book were written, Pastor Bryant directed a prayer that this book would reach countless people and that those who read would experience Jesus Christ unlike ever before. That they would immediately come to know God's power like the characters mentioned, and upon reading people would have their hope restored, their faith renewed, their healing granted and their hearts entwined with that of their loving Savior.

Thank you Pastor Michael Bryant for your prayers and continued faithfulness. Because of them I remained steadfast, and this book found its completion

CONTENTS

DUNAMIS

Greek: δύναμις, εως, ἡ

Definition: (**Miraculous**) Power, Might, Strength

Strong's Concordance 1411

ɷ NOW HE 'NOSE' ɷ

Our first story begins one spring afternoon on Long Island, New York. John was an extremely active thirteen year old boy, usually coming home with scrapes, sprains and the occasional broken bone from one of his many activities, the most recent being a member of his junior high wrestling team. He excelled at everything he did including wrestling. However, during one of his matches his opponent inadvertently collided his elbow with John's already twice broken nose, resulting in a seriously deviated septum. It was roughly two weeks before the swelling subsided and although John wasn't experiencing any pain, he was left with severe congestion and a very noticeable bend to his nose. Even so, not even a deviated septum would keep him from his wrestling.

One afternoon John returned from school to find his mother folding clothes in front of the television. John's parents were originally opposed to the purchase of the TV, but once aware of the available Christian channels, they decided to try it. So it wasn't uncommon for Christian television to be on in their house. This particular afternoon, John walked in and his mother was watching the "700 Club." He greeted his mother and turned his attention to the television. The man on the screen was speaking on healing and began to pray for those God impressed upon his heart. As the man prayed, John began to smirk and soon the smirk turned into a chuckle of disbelief. His mirth was silenced, however, when the man started praying for someone with a deviated septum. John's eyes grew wide and he yelled in amazement to his mother, sitting on the couch, that his nose and face felt like they were on fire. Shortly after his nose began to run steadily for over an hour. They both stared at the man on the television as he continued to pray. By now, John had laser focus on every word that came out of this man's mouth. A little over an hour later, his sister Maureen came home. At first look, also amazed, she acknowledged his nose was no longer deformed. John claimed to have felt the heat of God's healing presence on his face for the rest of that day. This would be the first of many miracles that God would perform on John's behalf and other than a small bump left as a reminder of this miraculous event in his life, he now had a perfect nose.

JESUS WALKS ON THE SEA

Immediately Jesus made His disciples get into the boat and go before Him to the other side, while He sent the multitudes away. And when He had sent the multitudes away, He went up on the mountain by Himself to pray. Now when evening came, He was alone there. But the boat was now in the middle of the sea, tossed by the waves, for the wind was contrary.

Now in the fourth watch of the night Jesus went to them, walking on the sea. And when the disciples saw Him walking on the sea, they were troubled, saying, "It is a ghost!" And they cried out for fear.

But immediately Jesus spoke to them, saying, "Be of good cheer! It is I; do not be afraid."

And Peter answered Him and said, "Lord, if it is You, command me to come to You on the water."

So He said, "Come." And when Peter had come down out of the boat, he walked on the water to go to Jesus. But when he saw that the wind was boisterous, he was afraid; and beginning to sink he cried out, saying, "Lord, save me!"

And immediately Jesus stretched out His hand and caught him, and said to him, "O you of little faith, why did you doubt?" And when they got into the boat, the wind ceased.

Then those who were in the boat came and worshiped Him, saying, "Truly You are the Son of God."

Matthew 14:22-33 (NKJV)

ɑ COUNTING ON DIGITS ɑ

She was only twelve years old, yet what happened one morning would remain one of the greatest demonstrations of Jesus Christ's power. It would mark a major event in the history of her life that she could always look back to when she needed reassurance of just how much God truly cares for her.

The house her parents purchased was originally built in the late 1960s. So, when they moved into the home in the early 80s, they knew what they were getting. Even though it wasn't the biggest or even the newest home, Maureen's parents did everything they could, with their limited budget, to try to give their children the best they had to offer. For so many people living in such a small house, it was hard, but her parents were fully determined to make it work. They knew it would be possible as long as God remained their primary focus.

Part of making this work was by everyone pitching in and helping when needed. On this particular day, Maureen helped by doing the laundry. After breakfast, Maureen made her way down the rickety, old, wooden stairs to the basement from the kitchen. Sitting in the far left corner was the old, but reliable washing machine. Unlike most machines nowadays, which drain into a sewer or cesspool, their machine drained into a dry well located in the center of their basement. A hose ran across the cement floor and under the, slightly propped up, heavy round cover that capped the well.

Maureen carefully balanced herself on the little wooden stool while placing the first load of sorted clothing into the top loader machine. She turned the dial and pulled the knob. Water filled the machine as she meticulously measured the soap, poured it in and closed the cover. Now with the first load started, she made her way back up to the kitchen to help her mother while the clothes ran through their cycle.

Twenty minutes later Maureen went back down to the basement to check on the laundry. Once again, she carefully stepped on the stool, opened the top to the machine and looked inside. Noticing the water didn't look like it was draining from the machine, she jumped off her stool and followed the hose running across the floor to the dry well. In an attempt to see whether the machine was actually draining, Maureen managed to pry up the heavy cover. It was in this moment that what started out as a seemingly ordinary day would turn just the opposite.

While attempting to lift the cover she lost her grip and the cover slammed, with all its weight, onto her right index finger. From the kitchen, her mother heard screams coming from the basement unlike anything she had ever heard before. There was such distress in this scream that her mother suddenly dropped what she was doing and ran down the stairs. Maureen's cousins, Steven and Justin, also ran in from outside once they heard the commotion. At the bottom of the stairs, Maureen's mother found her screaming in horror as she held her bloodied hand outstretched. Without thought and what she admits was the quickening of the Holy Spirit, Maureen's mother grabbed her hand and quickly raced Maureen up the stairs into the kitchen. As she was being sprinted across the kitchen to the sink, Steven and Justin were paralyzed with disbelief as they caught sight of her finger. What could only be described as chopped meat from a butcher, what little remained of Maureen's finger was unrecognizable.

Still under the quickening of the Holy Spirit, Maureen's mother turned on the cold water, pushed her finger under it and spoke the words, "Be healed in Jesus' name." Once these words were spoken, Steven and Justin's disbelief over Maureen's finger turned to amazement at the sight of her now healed finger! In an instant Maureen's finger was healed with no evidence that anything had ever happened. On that day, God showed not only Maureen, but all who were present just what a miraculous God He really is.

JESUS HEALS ON THE SABBATH

At that time Jesus went through the grainfields on the Sabbath. His disciples were hungry and began to pick some heads of grain and eat them. When the Pharisees saw this, they said to Him, "Look! Your disciples are doing what is unlawful on the Sabbath."

He answered, "Haven't you read what David did when he and his companions were hungry? He entered the house of God, and he and his companions ate the consecrated bread—which was not lawful for them to do, but only for the priests. Or haven't you read in the Law that the priests on Sabbath duty in the temple desecrate the Sabbath and yet are innocent? I tell you that something greater than the temple is here. If you had known what these words mean, 'I desire mercy, not sacrifice,' you would not have condemned the innocent. For the Son of Man is Lord of the Sabbath."

Going on from that place, He went into their synagogue, and a man with a shriveled hand was there. Looking for a reason to bring charges against Jesus, they asked him, "Is it lawful to heal on the Sabbath?"

He said to them, "If any of you has a sheep and it falls into a pit on the Sabbath, will you not take hold of it and lift it out? How much more valuable is a person than a sheep! Therefore, it is lawful to do good on the Sabbath."

Then He said to the man, "Stretch out your hand." So he stretched it out and it was completely restored, just as sound as the other.

Matthew 12:1-13 (NIV)

Ꙫ HE'S GOT MY BACK Ꙫ

There are many revelations we discover about God every day, but it seems the more we find, the more remains to be discovered. If there are three things you discover by the end of this book, they are that miracles come in all shapes and sizes, however, no one less profound from the other. Every miracle is tailored by God Himself for your individual needs. Lastly, some miracles are immediate, while others require a steadfast heart waiting on the promise to come to pass. Which was exactly the case in Pastor Sonny's testimony.

September 24, 2010

If rusty nails were slowly driven through his bones, taking their time to rub up against every nerve resulting in deep, debilitating unbearable pain, this still wouldn't compare to the agony Pastor Sonny experienced for years, as he continued to wait on a promise given to him by God. Sitting in his chair trying not to move, his thoughts most likely resembled the obvious. While taking every second to dismiss them in hopes of focusing on the healing virtue of Jesus Christ and what He promised just a year earlier.

Winter 1996

Stepping off the plane, he was glad to be home. However, his excitement wasn't enough to keep him from noticing the pain in his lower stomach. What could possibly be attributed to food poisoning or maybe a food-borne pathogen, he thought he practiced all food safety measures on this trip to Haiti. Maybe something slipped through? Perhaps it will get better in a few days?

A few days had passed and the pain grew worse. By the third day the pain was so unbearable that Pastor Sonny drove himself to the Emergency Room, despite the knife stabbing pain that shot through his lower abdomen with every bump and turn. The doctor made the obvious assumption that he had picked up something while on his past trip, but decided to run various tests just to be positive. After the results came back, the doctor reached his diagnosis. His original assumptions weren't conclusive, however, what was obvious was that Pastor Sonny may be suffering from acute diverticulitis. The attending physician immediately called in a gastroenterologist, by the name of Dr. E.C, to perform a colonoscopy in hopes of narrowing down the underlying issue.

When Dr. E.C. attempted to perform the procedure, it became quickly apparent that it couldn't be done. He told Sonny, "We are unable to perform the procedure today because your intestines are too inflamed. We will proceed when the swelling subsides." He wrote Pastor Sonny two prescriptions that would aid in alleviating the swelling and scheduled another appointment.

The day before the procedure, Sonny received a call to confirm his appointment with Dr. E.C. Feeling much better, he was almost tempted to cancel. Nevertheless, because of that still small voice and that of his wife's, he decided he would keep it just to be sure everything was alright.

The day had arrived and thankfully the swelling subsided enough to have the doctor perform the procedure. Once the procedure was completed, Pastor Sonny was given some time to come out of the anesthesia. After which, he and his wife met with the doctor to discuss what was discovered.

Waiting in the doctor's office, Pastor Sonny grabbed his wife's hand and slightly squeezed it as he turned towards her and reassured her that God had everything under control. Dr. E.C. entered, sat on his chair and proceeded to tell them that everything went normal; however, they did find polyps and so suspicions were confirmed that he had diverticulitis. The doctor said, "I'm extremely glad we were able to perform the procedure today, because in the process we removed a massive polyp." They both gave a big sigh of relief as he read through the pathology report. "Your polyp shows no signs of malignancy," he stated. It must have been the Holy Spirit, because with no reason for further examination the doctor decided he would personally dissect the polyp just to make sure nothing was overlooked, and would be in contact once he knew anything. Pastor Sonny and his wife left the doctor's office believing that the Lord answered their prayers and the worst was over.

@

Lifting the fork to his mouth he gently blew on and tasted the pasta. "Just perfect". It was roughly 5 p.m. while Pastor Sonny and his wife were in the middle of serving their children dinner when the phone began to ring. "Who could be calling us during dinner?" Fran picked up the phone.

"Hello?"

"This is Doctor E.C., is Sonny Available?"

"He's right here, one second please."

She handed the phone to her husband and told him it was the Doctor. All was quiet in the kitchen.

"Hello."

"Hi Sonny, I apologize for calling so late but it is extremely important that I see you immediately."

"Ok – Should I call your office and schedule an appointment for some time this week?"

"No, you need to come in right away, can you make it here tonight?"

"We will be there as soon as we finish serving the children dinner."

Once Sonny finished his call he told Fran, "The doctor would like to see us in his office immediately." It was as if all the air was sucked from the room. Looking at each other, there was an obvious feeling of apprehension. – *After all, no good can come from your doctor telling you he needs to see you immediately.-*

The ride to the doctor's office was filled with the worst case scenarios playing over in their minds; only interrupted by continual reassurances from each other that God had everything under control. Once at the office the doctor brought them in right away.

"As you know, when the original pathology report came back negative, I just had an overwhelming suspicion that I should examine the polyp further. As I began to cut into the polyp all seemed normal, but as I cut deeper that's when I discovered a problem. I found abnormal cells and sent another sample to the pathologist. I'm sorry to tell you this, but it was cancerous."

Even though this thought was sitting in the back of their minds from the time they received his call, no one can predict how they will feel or react when those actual words are spoken. After all, it was no more than five years prior when Pastor Sonny's wife had to go through a hard struggle with cancer herself. Pastor Sonny later said, "I felt as if someone had driven a dagger through my stomach when the doctor gave us the news." So, what do you do when your worst fears are confirmed?

She reached over and grabbed his hand as silence filled the office for roughly ten seconds. They exchanged a glance, reading each other's faces the silence was broken when Fran asked, "What do you suggest we do from here?"

The doctor replied, "It would be my recommendation that you have surgery to remove the affected area of your intestine where the cancer was found. At the same time we would also completely remove the area affected by the diverticulitis."

Many other questions were exchanged during that visit. However, both Sonny and Fran agreed with Dr. E.C. that surgery was the best solution. Wrapping up the visit, the Doctor asked, "Do you have a preferred surgeon? If not I could recommend one."

Immediately, Fran said, "If at all possible we would like Dr. C.B." This was the doctor that performed her surgery years earlier.

"I'll get in touch with the surgeon and schedule the surgery. In the meantime, if you have any questions please call anytime."

@

The day of the surgery arrived and anxiety filled the air. Pastor Sonny had been admitted to the hospital the day before and spent most of the day taking various tests in preparation for this morning's surgery. His wife prayed with him one last time, and assured him that God had everything under control, after which, he was wheeled into the operating room.

-The prayers of many were with Pastor Sonny that day. Family, friends, Church family and thousands of people in Haiti all sent up continual prayers on his behalf. -

During the surgery, Dr. C.B. removed over 18 inches of infected intestine, completely removing the areas affected by the cancer, as well as that which had the diverticulitis. During the lengthy surgery the surgeon also discovered a hernia which he repaired. Overall, the surgery went as routinely as such an intricate surgery could go. However, immediately post-surgery Pastor Sonny couldn't even savor his successful operation because of an adverse reaction to his medication.

A few days later, on his birthday, Pastor Sonny was considered stable enough to be released from the hospital. Recovery was slow and arduous, however he and his wife continually gave God glory for getting them through this time. This was an incredibly strong learning experience for Pastor Sonny. It was a lesson on putting your complete faith in God and resting in the security that He has everything under control. This would be exactly the type of faith that he would need for what awaited him just around the corner.

Spring 2006

Sitting in another waiting room he found himself, once again, waiting to be called in to see the doctor. What brought him into the office this time was a serious case of indigestion. When over the counter relief would no longer help he thought perhaps the family doctor could, so he decided to schedule an appointment. Meticulously explaining to the doctor the exact discomfort he was feeling, the doctor didn't suspect anything out of the ordinary. However, seeing it was a while since Sonny's last full checkup, the doctor suggested they do one this time. Following a full physical, Pastor Sonny was sent to have blood labs done. The Doctor said, "As soon as your labs come in we will be in contact."

Pastor Sonny and his wife had an out of town engagement; but when they returned, awaiting them was an urgent letter from their doctor which stated that they had tried numerous times to contact him, and it was important that he call the office as soon as possible. Accompanying that letter were letters from three different specialists. His family practitioner had taken it upon himself to schedule these appointments hoping he could be seen promptly. "This can't be good." Unfortunately they would have to wait until Monday to find out more.

One can only imagine the anxiety that Sonny and his wife felt having to wait a whole weekend for what could be more devastating news. However, because of what Pastor Sonny had already gone through, anxiety and fear didn't have the same hold as it once did. God would remain his focus and a firm understanding that God had everything under control would be his rest.

Monday morning finally arrived and as soon as the office opened he was able to talk to the doctor. The doctor explained that he was very concerned with his test results and so took it upon himself to schedule appointments with three specialists. From what he gathered from the various tests, Pastor Sonny would need to see a cardiothoracic specialist for his heart, a urologist for his prostate and another specialist for an aortic aneurism.

Summer 2006

The first specialist he went to see was the cardiothoracic specialist. Pastor Sonny had additional tests performed and they were conclusive that he would need quadruple bypass surgery. Unfortunately, because of the extreme blockage of the arteries, this was the only option. They scheduled the surgery for a day in June 2006.

The day of the surgery arrived and once again his wife, joined by thousands of people from around the world, sent him off with prayers. However, this time would be different because one of the people joining in would be Pastor Sonny himself. Unlike his previous anxiety filled experience, this time was filled with peace. Even as he was being wheeled into surgery he continued to pray and praise God.

Imagine what the surgeons were thinking as they heard this man singing praises to God as the anesthesia took effect!

This surgery was quite extensive, after all, they would be rerouting four major blood vessels to the life pump of the body; the heart. Going in through a fourteen-inch incision in his chest, they meticulously bypassed arteries using blood vessels they had taken from his legs. This was quite an amazing thing considering they managed to do this while keeping his heart beating. As he was coming out of the anesthesia the first words that came out of his mouth were

"Praise God". From the time he went in, to the time he came out of the anesthesia his praises didn't miss a beat. All went incredibly well during the lengthy surgery and he was released from the hospital four days later with strict instructions; should he have any problems to come in right away.

Recovery took a while. If you had the chance to see Pastor Sonny after his surgery, you would have noticed the huge incision where they accessed the heart and the pins in his legs from where they harvested the vessels. This was no simple surgery, but once again, God had brought him through. With the help of God and his family he was able to recover and for the first time in many years, he felt amazing.

Prior to the Quadruple Bypass

The second person he saw was a specialist for what looked like an aggressive form of prostate cancer. The Urologist came in, sat him down and said, "You have advanced stage prostate cancer, hopefully we can find a treatment which may buy you some time." Pastor Sonny left the office and never returned. That night he discussed what the doctor said with his wife. They both agreed that they weren't going to accept it, that God was in control and that they would find a doctor who wouldn't be so quick to speak death into someone's life.

Fall 2006

Dr. T.R. to this day has been no less than someone sent by God and through this relationship God has been able to work in miraculous ways. God would ultimately give Sonny a special word for Dr. T.R. One spoken of him being used to help countless people. A word which Sonny would quickly see come to fruition.

Receiving all test results from the previous doctors, Dr. T.R. decided to see it for himself and have the tests redone. When the results came back Dr. T.R. had to admit the cancer was extremely aggressive and that Pastor Sonny must begin treatment right away. Treatment was meant to be started in September of 2006. However, Pastor Sonny told Dr. T.R. that he made a commitment to the people in Haiti and asked if he could start treatment once he returned. Against his better judgement, the doctor agreed.

Around this same time he had to follow up with his cardiologist Dr. D.M. to make sure everything was continuing to heal properly. During this visit the doctor addressed the aortic aneurism, however he felt it might be too soon to go back under the knife; not to mention, there was the whole end stage cancer diagnosis.

Imagine countless doctors trying to coordinate different tests, procedures and operations. Now try to imagine how Pastor Sonny was able to undergo everything. It was nothing short of

God working in all aspects of his situation. Providing grace when grace was needed and providing strength when strength was required.

Following his trip to Haiti, Pastor Sonny was referred to an oncologist by Dr. T.R. The treatment that Sonny, his wife and the oncologist agreed would be best would be radiation treatment. From November 2006 to January 2007, Pastor Sonny would receive the maximum dosage permitted for the most days allowed to be treated. Even during the treatment, in seeing how aggressive the cancer was, the oncologist and most other doctors routinely spoke phrases which encompassed words such as "hopefully" and "buying time". However, Pastor Sonny's trust was firmly in the Lord.

Towards the end of his radiation treatments, Sonny began to feel pain in his lower back and hips, and every passing day that pain grew worse. Following the radiation, Pastor Sonny was also given a course of hormone suppression therapy. One of the known side effects was the possibility of developing severe osteoporosis. When Pastor Sonny explained his pain to the doctor, the doctor had other suspicions and gave him another lab prescription. Not knowing what the test was for, Sonny and his wife went on their computer and researched it. The test was for bone cancer. Without coming out and saying it, it was evident that the doctor feared the cancer had metastasized to his bones. Pastor Sonny and his wife simultaneously agreed that they should not have the test done and God would continue to guide them through this time of trial.

Fall 2007

November 2007, Pastor Sonny met once again with his cardiothoracic specialist, Dr. J.H. This meeting was to discuss the aortic aneurism. Additional tests would determine with absolute certainty he would need another invasive surgery to address this issue, because his blood vessels were too obstructed to do it by any other means. This being the case, no surgeons were willing to perform the operation because of fear he would die on the operating table. When Doctor J.H. was made aware that no one would do the surgery, he got infuriated and said, "I told them that you were cleared for the procedure." Soon after, the cardiothoracic specialist recommended he travel to Shands Hospital. He mentioned that they were cutting edge and that they would have the best surgeons to perform such a procedure. They scheduled the surgery and Pastor Sonny began all the testing in preparation for the procedure.

Shands, although an exceptional hospital, was extremely far from where Pastor Sonny lived. He made every appointment that was scheduled but a time came when he felt he didn't want to subject his wife or children to driving him to the hospital as often as they were. So, he met once again with his cardiothoracic doctor and told him, "If I'm going to have a procedure done I will have it closer to home." He cancelled the surgery and decided that God would make a way.

In December 2007, unexpectedly, Pastor Sonny received a call from an unknown doctor. This doctor said that he was affiliated with Shands Hospital and after reviewing his chart, he believed he could perform the stent procedure thus avoiding having another major surgery. He understood why the previous surgeons had reservations, however he was fairly confident it could be done. He said, "Because your vessels are extremely obstructed, it is indeed an extremely high risk procedure, however if you would like to, I will perform it for you." Pastor Sonny agreed to have the procedure; After all, God brought this surgeon to him and what better person to trust than that handpicked by the Lord Himself. They scheduled the Procedure for later that month.

The day of the procedure came and, like the other times, Sonny's wife spent a significant time in prayer with him. This was going to be a little different than that of his past procedures. Unlike the others where he had anesthesia, this time he would have no such luxury. Because of his extremely obstructed vessels it was important that he be conscious the whole time and that required him lying painfully still on his back through the whole procedure. To make matters worse, just in the few days leading up to this procedure the bone pain in Sonny's lower back and hips had reached a whole new level.

The doctor paid careful attention in maneuvering the stent through extremely clogged vessels to address the aortic aneurism located by his kidney. The procedure took longer than a typical stent procedure, but the end result was incredible. Where all other surgeons spelt almost certain death, God spelt success through the hands of this doctor. Nevertheless, following this procedure Pastor Sonny would experience a test of faith unlike anything he had ever had to endure in his life.

@

The pain was immediate and intense, unlike anything he had ever felt before. "It felt like I was in a car crash and every bone in my body had shattered." Such intense deep sharp throbbing bone pain seemed impossible. During the lengthy procedure, Pastor Sonny had to remain as still as possible laying on his back and from the moment he got up from that table, terrible pain ensued. Lying in a hospital bed, trying not to move, he asked the doctor for something for the pain. The doctor kindly responded, "I'm sorry, but we cannot give you any more." Pastor Sonny continually reached out to God asking for some relief, but it didn't come. Extreme exhaustion riddled his body, but because of the intense pain he found no sleep. At 2:00 in the morning he reached over in agony on the verge of tears and picked up the phone. On the other end was a wife that wished if only for a second she could trade places to provide her husband some relief. Praying, talking and singing; Fran did everything she could to keep his mind from the pain. Three hours later, over exhausted from that pain, Sonny finally fell asleep. It was everyone's prayer that Pastor Sonny's pain would diminish with time, but the pain only intensified.

He was allowed to go home a few days after the procedure. On the ride home from the hospital, every bump in the road had Sonny reliving those moments after getting off the operating table. Once again brought to the brink of tears, he made it home. The walk from the driveway to the house might as well have been ten miles. With each step shooting pain ran up his body; spurring him on was the thought of his recliner bringing some relief. Finally sitting in that recliner, he realized the relief was nothing more than a mirage. His family looked on helplessly at the complete state of agony Pastor Sonny clearly was in.

What could a son, daughter or even a wife do to ease such suffering?

He was a paratrooper, a veteran who served in Korea, a businessman, devoted husband and father, and a Pastor who operated in the fivefold gifts of the Spirit; he was Christ's and now here he lay broken and exhausted.

The sight of Sonny in his recliner became normal. As if this intense pain wasn't enough, what made it worse was that Pastor Sonny had to endure this for a whole two years. It was two years of complete agony. Two years of missing out on spending time with his family. Two years of having to rely on family for help, but two years where he kept Jesus at the forefront of his thoughts. Anyone in such a state would probably remember and rehearse in their mind that day when the doctor thought it might be wise to test for bone cancer. Anyone in his state may even ask God to take them home. He continually reminded himself, "God got me through the bypass surgery, He's getting me through the prostate cancer, He found me a doctor to get me through the aortic aneurism, and now, He will not fail me."

September 25, 2009

September 25th of 2009 marked a very special day in Pastor Sonny and his wife's life. On this Friday morning everything started out as usual. Pastor Sonny, like every morning, made the coffee and brought a cup to his wife in bed; after which, he assumed the usual spot in the brown recliner which sat at the edge of their room. Before the start of every morning, Sonny and his wife spent hours praying for every family member, friend and church family by name. Following prayers, they would do their morning devotions and listen to praise and worship music. Nothing held more importance then giving God the first fruits of their day.

Over a year since he initially started having pain, Pastor Sonny still found little relief. Painkillers helped but were short lived and unfortunately homeopathic remedies didn't do much either. To add insult to injury, Sonny also suffered from gout which left his toe unbearably painful and swollen.

It's an extremely discouraging moment when you resign yourself to live in agony and yet every part of your being holds onto hope that God will perform a miracle on your behalf.

Extremely exhausted from little sleep from the night before, he sipped at his coffee in his recliner as his wife began to pray. Following her prayer, his wife began her morning devotions. About ten minutes into her devotions, she heard the small quiet voice of the Holy Spirit directing her to Isaiah 58. As she began to read through the chapter, her spirit became uplifted. What God had directed her to was a promise of her husband's healing. Immediately she called to Sonny, "Hey Sonny."

"Yes Hun?"

"God just showed me a healing! He showed me this is a word for you."

Sonny listened intently at every word as she read, and as she read further into his promise, joy began to fill his heart. By the end of verse 9 he was brought to tears.

5 Is it a fast that I have chosen, a day for a man to afflict his soul? Is it to bow down his head like a bulrush, And to spread out sackcloth and ashes? Would you call this a fast, and an acceptable day to the Lord? 6 "Is this not the

fast that I have chosen: To loose the bonds of wickedness, to undo the heavy burdens, to let the oppressed go free, and that you break every yoke? 7 Is it not to share your bread with the hungry, And that you bring to your house the poor who are cast out; When you see the naked, that you cover him, And not hide yourself from your own flesh? 8 Then your light shall break forth like the morning, your healing shall spring forth speedily, and your righteousness shall go before you; the glory of the Lord shall be your rear guard. 9 Then you shall call, and the Lord will answer; you shall cry, and He will say, 'Here I am.'

Isaiah 58:5-9 (NKJV)

After reading, she continued by asking:

"Has not your whole life been about this fast? The countless people you've helped feed and clothed in Haiti and here at home. Have you not provided shelter to many who have been in need, also, many times, taking them into your own home? Has God not used you to help loosen the burdens of many people?"

Sonny couldn't help but smile. The joy of the Lord and His presence filled the room in that moment, an experience that seemed a distant memory. From that morning until the time God fulfilled this promise, they stood firm on the promise that Sonny's healing would indeed spring forth.

September 26, 2010

It had been a year since God originally gave Sonny his promise and not a single day had passed without, both him and his wife, actively waiting for the day when he would be healed. Like every other night, Pastor Sonny struggled to get to and remain asleep; constantly tossing and turning because laying in one position would exaggerate the pain.

Because of his prostate, it was pretty routine for him to get up often during the night to use the bathroom. Imagine for one second finally falling asleep due to the exhaustion of pain and then being forced to wake up only hours later. This was the reality of Pastor Sonny's life for the past two years.

1:30 a.m. on the morning of September 26th 2010, Pastor Sonny dragged himself out of bed making his way towards the bathroom. He noticed something was amiss, but extremely tired he returned to bed giving no further thought to the matter. At 3:30 a.m. he, once again, made his way to and from the bathroom. But this time on his way back he took extensive notice that something was still amiss. Then all at once, on this Sunday morning, it hit him. He was healed.

The agonizing pain which plagued his body for over two years was suddenly gone. Overjoyed, it took everything he had in him not to awaken his wife. Slipping out of the bedroom quietly, he went to another part of the house where he began to praise God. For hours he walked back and forth through the room, bending down, raising his hands, dancing and praising before the Lord. When his wife woke up he immediately shared the good news. Both of them, extremely overjoyed, together rejoiced in the Lord.

December 2013

It had been over three years since God miraculously intervened on Pastor Sonny's behalf and not a day went by where he didn't devote part of his day to giving God the glory. All the trials and tribulations that Pastor Sonny had gone through have served to build up an undeniable faith in the Lord Jesus Christ. This is a faith that goes beyond what doctors may say. This is a faith that goes beyond how one may feel. This is a faith that is firmly planted in the Lord Jesus Christ as the sole source for everything that one may want and need. It is one that can lay to rest our deepest fears and anxieties; a faith that can provide hope given any situation.

Now faith is the substance of things hoped for, the evidence of things not seen

-Hebrews 11:1 (KJV)

The Final Test

In December 2013, Sonny was due to have his stent checked. This was something routinely done as a precaution.

What seemed was going to be another non-eventful C.T. scan would be anything but.

Dr. T.R. would, once again, bear the responsibility of breaking devastating news to Sonny. But just to be sure, he ordered additional testing before he reached his diagnosis. His exact words were, "I want to see it for myself." His tests were conclusive and damning. During the C.T. scan doctors had found a large mass on his ureter and further testing by Dr. T.R., found it to be malignant and extremely aggressive. It would be a pretty accurate assumption that if the cancer hadn't already, it would soon spread to his kidney. Once again in Dr. T.R.'s office, Dr. T.R. explained that the cancer found this time spreads extremely fast and should be removed immediately. It would take two separate surgeries. Sitting across from the doctor, Pastor Sonny asked, "If I were not to have the surgery, how long would I have?"

"I'm sorry Sonny, but the most you would have is one, maybe two years."

Pastor Sonny had him schedule the surgeries for after his return from Haiti.

Because Pastor Sonny and his wife were leaving for Haiti the next day, they were extremely busy getting ready for their trip. So much so that they didn't have the opportunity to discuss the news the doctor recently gave them.

We assume most people given a death sentence would be completely devastated; and how simply being preoccupied with something so inconsequential wouldn't ordinarily be enough to divert the reality of the situation. However what would, is the knowledge and the forming of an innate trust in God based on His past provisions in your life.

The five hour ride to the airport finally gave them time to evaluate what the doctor had told them the day before. Much of the time was spent coming before the Lord in prayer, over what seemed to be another attack on Pastor Sonny's life. Even though the surgeries were already scheduled, Sonny and Fran now had the opportunity to discuss whether or not surgery should actually be something to consider. After much discussion and prayer, they stood together in agreement trusting that God would clearly show them, by the end of this trip, which direction to take.

The Answer Awaits in Haiti

There has never been one trip to Haiti where God hasn't moved in a supernatural way and this trip was no exception. During the week that Pastor Sonny and Fran were there, they held services four days of the week. For those four days Sonny and Fran preached to the congregation, helped with missions work and spent time with individuals who needed prayer. On Thursday night, following Pastor

Sonny's message, the whole congregation came together to pray over him and his wife.

Immediately as the congregation began praying, Sonny and Fran felt countless hands being laid upon them. Clearly the presence of God was there and He was going to do something amazing. Of all the hands that were laid on Pastor Sonny, surprisingly none were laid on his head or feet. Roughly twenty-five minutes into the prayers, Pastor Sonny heard God speak to him. The Lord said, "Sonny, do not have the surgery, I will keep you." Inwardly, Sonny spoke the words, "I claim this healing from the crown of my head to the soles of my feet." In the moment that he inwardly spoke the words "crown of my head" countless hands were laid upon his head and the instant that he inwardly spoke "soles of my feet" hands descended upon his feet. Immediately he knew, without a doubt, God was going to keep him.

Back Home

Once back in Florida, Sonny met once again with Dr. T.R. One could only imagine what was going through his mind when Sonny said he wasn't going to have the surgery. Then again, Dr. T.R. had personally seen the hand of God work many times on Sonny's behalf. So, who's to know exactly what he was thinking. Nevertheless, Pastor Sonny explained what took place a week prior in Haiti and although he had reservations, the doctor agreed on one condition.

That condition required Pastor Sonny agreeing to come in for periodic examinations and should the cancer get worse, they would go ahead with treatment.

January 2017

Dr. T.R. walked into the exam room with test results in hand. Sonny looked up to find a huge smile on the doctor's face. "It's been three years," he said never breaking his smile. Smiling back, Sonny replied, "I told you, the Lord has been very faithful." As Dr. T.R. began discussing his test results, it became quickly apparent that this just may be one of the most unique visits to this office that Sonny has ever had. From the time that God sent Dr. T.R. into Sonny's life, or vice versa one could argue, every visit has involved managing and treating the catastrophe that was Pastor Sonny's body. This visit was to the contrary. All his test results came back amazing, the mass located next to his kidney hadn't spread, in fact, it appeared to have shrunken. Clearly the joy of the Lord now filled every part of his being. The doctor even went so far as to lightheartedly say, "It may not be necessary to have you continue your periodic examinations." Leaving the doctor's office that day, Pastor Sonny knew beyond a shadow of a doubt that regardless of anything that may happen in this life, nothing can separate us from God's eternal love.

Yet in all these things we are more than conquerors through Him who loved us. For I am persuaded that neither death nor life, nor angels nor principalities nor powers, nor things present nor things to come, nor height nor depth, nor any other created thing, shall be able to separate us from the love of God which is in Christ Jesus our Lord.

Romans 8:37-39 (NKJV)

JESUS RAISES LAZARUS FROM THE DEAD

Jesus, once more deeply moved, came to the tomb. It was a cave with a stone laid across the entrance. "Take away the stone," he said.

"But, Lord," said Martha, the sister of the dead man, "by this time there is a bad odor, for he has been there four days."

Then Jesus said, "Did I not tell you that if you believe, you will see the glory of God?"

So they took away the stone. Then Jesus looked up and said, "Father, I thank you that you have heard me. I know that you always hear me, but I said this for the benefit of the people standing here, that they may believe that you sent me."

When he had said this, Jesus called in a loud voice, "Lazarus, come out!" The dead man came out, his hands and feet wrapped with strips of linen, and a cloth around his face.

Jesus said to them, "Take off the grave clothes and let him go."

John 11:38-44 (NIV)

ꙍ SPECIAL K ꙍ

Looking back on this particular event, she remembers her life slowly fading. Past the moment of fear, a calming acceptance of the reality that within seconds she will fall asleep never to awake. Like drifting into a hollow tunnel, her vision slowly faded and her hearing became faint. *This is it,* she thought, as she resigned herself to passing. Reminiscent of slowly sinking under water, peacefully drifting away with the current; her life seems to escape her body. Just then she hears the door open and the faint sounds of her mother's voice.

Back to the Beginning

Lisa was extremely bright and independent. One could argue with all the possibilities in the world. A regular social butterfly and yet like most adolescents even the brightest individuals are capable of lapses in good judgement. This would be one lapse which would end in nothing short of a miracle.

This day started much the same as any other. Lisa got up, had some breakfast, and prepared for the day. She helped her mother with a few chores and then it was off to meet some friends. Unbeknownst to her parents, Lisa had kept another part of her life a secret. For the past several months Lisa had been partaking in recreational drugs. Behind a closed shopping center was the meeting place. Lisa and her friends would get together and whatever drugs were on hand would be the flavor of the day. Today's flavor was THC; or so she thought. Nothing like escaping life for a few hours through the hallucinogenic effects of THC.

She held out her hand while her friend pulled a single capsule from a paper bag and placed it in her palm. Since this wasn't her first experience, she was looking forward to escaping to a drug induced reality for a while. She placed the pill in her mouth, chased it with a soft drink and waited for the drug to take effect. Some time had passed and still no noticeable effect could be felt, so she swallowed another.

It wasn't hard to determine that her friends were already feeling the effects from the drugs. So why hadn't she? She once again reached into the bag and pulled out another pill. "Perhaps one more will do it?" The pill hadn't even hit her stomach when she began to feel the effects of the drugs.

Although, initially quite content with her high, she quickly realized something was amiss. Once the feeling went beyond what she had previously experienced, she became extremely concerned and made her way back home in hopes that someone there could help. Only God knows how she managed to make her way back, but she did. However, no one was home.

Stumbling through the front door with a river of tears running down her face, she made her way to her room. Stopping only for a few seconds to look in the mirror, mascara bleeding away from her eyes, her reflection now resembled something devilish. Completely exhausted she fell back onto her bed. Now staring at the ceiling she realized the gravity of her situation. Initially fear set in, soon accompanied by a feeling of helplessness. She felt as if she was sinking further and further into her bed, as if the bed were made of some gelatinous substance. Every second that passed might as well have been an hour. Time seemed to slow down, whereby giving her every possible opportunity to focus ón the fact that her life was passing. Then the time came.

Now seconds away from her final moment, she resigned herself to death, who seemed to wait patiently to claim what was his. Her breathing became shallower with every breath until finally, she closed her eyes and allowed death to take her. Just then she heard a door open. Almost completely unconscious and now with her breathing beginning to fail, it took every ounce of life left in her to cry out. "MOM!" This single word left her lips with little more than a whisper, with no guarantee her call was heard.

Just then the door to her bedroom swung open. All it took was one look at her daughter to know something was seriously wrong. She raced over and sat beside her on the bed. With every last ounce of energy she could muster, still nearly unconscious from the drugs, Lisa struggled to explain the day's events to her mother. Hastened by the Holy Spirit, the mother began to pray. With her right hand on Lisa's head, she boldly concluded her prayer "In the Name of Jesus - Amen." Lisa gasped and took in a deep breath. The Lord breathed a new breath of life into her failing body. She quickly regained consciousness. The color came back to her face and before her mother's eyes, Lisa was made well. Because of the healing blood of Jesus Christ, this was a time where death was left wanting.

ELIJAH AND ZAREPHATH'S WIDOW

...Sometime later, the son of the woman who owned the house became ill. He grew worse and worse, and finally stopped breathing. She said to Elijah, "What do you have against me, man of God? Did you come to remind me of my sin and kill my son?"

"Give me your son," Elijah replied. He took him from her arms, carried him to the upper room where he was staying, and laid him on his bed. Then he cried out to the LORD, "LORD my God, have you brought tragedy even on this widow I am staying with, by causing her son to die?" Then he stretched himself out on the boy three times and cried out to the LORD, "LORD my God, let this boy's life return to him!"

The LORD heard Elijah's cry, and the boy's life returned to him, and he lived. Elijah picked up the child and carried him down from the room into the house. He gave him to his mother and said, "Look, your son is alive!"

Then the woman said to Elijah, "Now I know that you are a man of God and that the word of the LORD from your mouth is the truth."

1 Kings 17:17-24 (NIV)

ɷ "I AM NO PROPHET" ɷ

It was the conclusion to another powerful message given at 'Eglise Communion De La Manne'. Following his message, Pastor Sonny was invited by Pastor, Reverend Roger 'Wilson' Charles, to his home for an early supper. Along with Pastor Sonny, Pastor Wilson also invited a few other members from his congregation. Over the years that Pastor Sonny and his wife had been visiting to Haiti, the people had become as close as family and from that time when Pastor Sonny and Fran were first introduced to Reverend Wilson, their history in the making has been filled with nothing short of God's constant supernatural involvement.

There is an amazing thing that happens when God's people come together. It doesn't matter if it's coming together to pray, to talk, or in this case, to eat. God is continually working through His people whether it's noticed or not. It is because of this that the miraculous seems to happen where and when it is least expected.

Pastor Sonny was sitting down enjoying a lovely home cooked meal when he heard a still small voice tell him to look across the table. On the other side of the table sat Wigins and his wife Marie-Lourdes. Wigins was an extremely devoted and faithful man, both towards his wife and even more so to the Lord; and although they didn't have much, everything they did have was used to bless others. Now it was their turn to be blessed.

After years of trying to no avail, Wigins and his wife were finally told that they would never be able to have a child. In spite of what the doctors said, they continued to try and trust that God would give them the desire of their hearts. But after many more years, seemingly all hope was lost. Although they continued to trust in God, not a second would go by without a reminder of what they would never have. Looking around at other families in the congregation created a sadness so painful and yet with the little remaining hope she had, Marie-Lourdes would muster the strength to pray to the Lord Jesus Christ for the blessing of a child. After ten long years of praying and pleading with the Lord, Marie-Lourdes became married to that deep sadness. That's when the Lord showed His heart for her.

As Pastor Sonny was sitting at the table the Lord began to speak. "Sonny, look at Marie-Lourdes." With his eyes focused on Marie-Lourdes, God began to share with him the great sadness that was in her heart. The Lord allowed Sonny to feel the heaviness and pain that plagued her for so many years. Shortly thereafter, that overwhelming feeling of sadness turned to joy and love as God began to show Pastor Sonny His heart for her. He sat back in his chair and said, "Lord, I'm listening, what would you have me do?"

The Lord said, "Sonny, the womb which many have said is dead, I will bring to life and she will bring forth a child."

"Lord, should I tell her now?"

"Wait until this evening's service. I want this to be a demonstration of My power and the love I have for her and all those who will bear witness tonight."

And so Pastor Sonny waited.

When the evening had arrived, Pastor Sonny began preaching the sermon he had put together earlier. All the while, patiently waiting for God to tell him when he should reveal what He had spoken earlier that day. Roughly an hour and a half into the message God spoke to Sonny. "Now is the time."

Pastor Wilson translated every word that Pastor Sonny spoke beginning with calling Marie-Lourdes forward to the front of the church. As Pastor Sonny began speaking, the church grew silent. Many in the congregation had a personal relationship with Wigins and Marie-Lourdes and knew of their struggle. After revealing to Wigins, Marie-Lourdes and the congregation what the Lord had spoken, Pastor Sonny called forward some of the women, including Pastor Wilson's wife, to pray over Marie-Lourdes. He continued by saying, "The Lord has brought to life Marie-Lourdes' dead womb and she will have a child, until the time this promise comes to pass be faithful to pray over Marie-Lourdes every night." A new sense of hope filled Wigin's and his wife's heart. A hope that seemed to have been lost somewhere in the years leading up to this moment. Many in the church began to praise and thank God for the miracle which was yet to come to pass. Then the Lord had Pastor Sonny say one last thing.

Just as Pastor Sonny was about finished with that evening's service, the Lord spoke to him once more and told him to say, "If that which I have spoken tonight does not come to pass, I am no Prophet." Whether because of fear, sadness or possibly a combination of both, following these last words, many approached Pastor Wilson and expressed their concerns. Understandably, their concern was if this thing which was spoken does not come to pass, this man that they had known and loved as one of the Lord's anointed and one of the spiritual heads of their church would be brought into question. This would be an outcome too unbearable for some. When approached, Pastor Wilson gave one simple answer, "Wait and see what the Lord will do."

It was three months later when his phone started ringing. Pastor Sonny reached across his desk and picked up the phone. On the other end of the line was Pastor Wilson.

"Hi, Brother Sonny."

"Hi Brother, how are you?"

"I have some great news to share with you."

"What's the news?"

"The word which was spoken came to pass, Sister Marie-Lourdes is pregnant."

That conversation was one of the most memorable moments of both Pastor Sonny's and Pastor Wilson's life. The Lord made a promise and brought to pass what He had promised. That phone call lasted over an hour as they continued to talk on the great things that the Lord had done and further encouraged each other that it wasn't the last time they would see the Lord act in such a way.

Nine months had passed and Pastor Sonny and Fran were once again in Haiti. This time was extremely special because it was the first opportunity they would have to see the child that God had promised. To the amusement of all those around, every time Pastor Sonny would hold the child she would cry. This Miracle child born only months earlier to Wigins and Marie-Lourdes; a beautiful baby girl named Ruth.

From Marie-Lourdes' countenance, there was no mistaking that love now filled that place where sadness used to occupy. God's joy seemed to radiate from her as if it were something contagious. The Lord had indeed done the impossible and with every opportunity Wigins and Marie-Lourdes were given, they gave God praise for this blessing. But the Lord wasn't quite done blessing them just yet.

On the last night of their visit, Pastor Sonny was preaching his last service before heading back to the States with his wife the next morning. Towards the end of his message the Lord, once again, began to speak to him. He turned towards Marie-Lourdes and Wigins, who were amongst the congregation and said, "That which the Lord has done once, He shall do again."

Over twenty years later, Wigins and Pastor Sonny were reminiscing on all the wonderful blessings the Lord was faithful to promise and bring to pass. Of all the promises, Wigins recalled a promise that the Lord spoke, through Pastor Sonny, well before he and his wife tried having children. This promise was that, "God will keep you and bless you and your family." Now every time he looks at his beautiful wife and four beautiful children, he can't help but acknowledge God's continual blessings upon his life. There is nothing that can convince him that the Lord is anything less than the God of the impossible.

HANNAH

There was a certain man from Ramathaim, a Zuphite from the hill country of Ephraim, whose name was Elkanah son of Jeroham, the son of Elihu, the son of Tohu, the son of Zuph, an Ephraimite. He had two wives; one was called Hannah and the other Peninnah. Peninnah had children, but Hannah had none.

Year after year this man went up from his town to worship and sacrifice to the LORD Almighty at Shiloh, where Hophni and Phinehas, the two sons of Eli, were priests of the LORD. Whenever the day came for Elkanah to sacrifice, he would give portions of the meat to his wife Peninnah and to all her sons and daughters. But to Hannah he gave a double portion because he loved her, and the LORD had closed her womb. Because the LORD had closed Hannah's womb, her rival kept provoking her in order to irritate her. This went on year after year. Whenever Hannah went up to the house of the LORD, her rival provoked her till she wept and would not eat. Her husband Elkanah would say to her, "Hannah, why are you weeping? Why don't you eat? Why are you downhearted? Don't I mean more to you than ten sons?"

Once when they had finished eating and drinking in Shiloh, Hannah stood up. Now Eli the priest was sitting on his chair by the doorpost of the LORD's house. In her deep anguish Hannah prayed to the LORD, weeping bitterly. And she made a vow, saying, "LORD Almighty, if you will only look on your servant's misery and remember me, and not forget your servant but give her a son, then I will give him to the LORD for all the days of his life, and no razor will ever be used on his head."

As she kept on praying to the LORD, Eli observed her mouth. Hannah was praying in her heart, and her lips were moving but her voice was not heard. Eli thought she was drunk and said to her, "How long are you going to stay drunk? Put away your wine."

"Not so, my Lord," Hannah replied. "I am a woman who is deeply troubled. I have not been drinking wine or beer; I was pouring out my soul to the LORD. Do not take your servant for a wicked woman; I have been praying here out of my great anguish and grief."

Eli answered, "Go in peace, and may the God of Israel grant you what you have asked of Him."

She said, "May your servant find favor in your eyes." Then she went her way and ate something, and her face was no longer downcast.

Early the next morning they arose and worshiped before the LORD and then went back to their home at Ramah. Elkanah made love to his wife Hannah, and the LORD remembered her. So in the course of time Hannah became pregnant and gave birth to a son. She named him Samuel, saying, "Because I asked the LORD for him."

1 Samuel 1:1-20 (NIV)

ɷ ALWAYS ON TIME ɷ

Placing one foot in front of the other, Rose slowly made her way down a narrow dirt Haitian road. She was still slightly bewildered as to the reason for her walking, yet something urged her to press on. Why was she walking? What had led her? Where was she going? All valid questions, yet the answer was still a mystery waiting to be revealed to her. What wasn't a mystery was that this long walk allowed her time to thoroughly think about her current situation and ponder the possible outcomes of her surgery the next morning.

Rose had been diagnosed with an extremely aggressive form of breast cancer and tomorrow would be the day that she would go under the knife. She had many apprehensions and myriad emotions continually flooded her mind. To make matters worse, with every visit to the doctors their prognosis seemed to become grimmer. However, for some reason there was some solace while she walked today. This same thing that urged and directed her to press on also, in some unknown way, granted her some comfort from the anxiety swirling around in her mind. Then she arrived.

She slowly lifted her head and about twenty-feet in front of her stood a building. It was a church. She stood still for a minute and watched from a distance the many people standing outside waiting to get in. She knew this was where she was meant to be, the place that she had been walking towards this whole time. She made her way towards the church doors and quickly noticed that those people standing outside the front doors weren't waiting to get in, but rather the church was so crowded that the congregation spilled out into the street. Managing to make her way inside the church, she now stood amongst many and intently listening as this American Pastor began his message. He introduced himself as Pastor Sonny and from what she could gather it wasn't the first time he had been there. The longer she listened, the more she knew that this was a special place and that the man speaking was sent of God.

With Bible in hand, Pastor Sonny walked back and forth across the front of the church delivering the message the Lord had placed upon his heart. All in the congregation were rapt. The very presence of the Lord could be felt throughout the church. Standing there, amidst the people, one could anticipate that something amazing was going to happen. Then that moment had arrived. With congregation looking on, Pastor Sonny grew silent, it wasn't a momentary lapse in thought, nor was it a pause to catch his breath. This was something different and Rose knew it.

He was roughly thirty minutes into his message when the Lord began to speak. Standing there before the congregation, the Lord told him, "There is someone I brought here tonight. She is afflicted with breast cancer and tonight is the night of her healing." Pastor Sonny, being respectful as to whether it was acceptable to mention a woman's breast amidst the congregation, asked Pastor Wilson if it would be ok. He responded, "It is alright, do what the Lord would have you." Pastor Sonny began to speak out into the congregation of what the Lord had placed upon his heart. Pastor Wilson meticulously translated every word that Pastor Sonny spoke and once finished, a woman came forward.

Weaving in and out of the crowd, Rose made her way to the front of the church. Once she had arrived, Pastor Sonny called for all the elders of the church to come forward and pray over her. The congregation extended their hands forward and stood in agreement as the elders' prayers were uttered. When the elders were finished, God, once again, spoke to Pastor Sonny and said, "Tell her to come back tomorrow and give her testimony. That which I have done for her I will also do for others." Pastor Sonny spoke these things to her and with all of her heart she held steadfastly onto every word. Now with promises spoken, Pastor Sonny, the elders and congregation greatly anticipated the next night's service.

This marked a very important visit to Haiti for many reasons. Most crucially, this particular visit would fall on the anniversary of the church. The way in which God provided the property and building was a miracle itself. But that's a story for another time. During this visit, Pastor Wilson held church services every night and during these mini-revival services people from far and wide came to this church. It was clearly God that drew them because many would find themselves standing in front of the church with no other reason than feeling a need to be there.

The next night had arrived and like most other nights, time was set aside at the outset of the evening for people to give their testimonies. A small woman came forward from the crowd. It was Rose, and she was ready to give her testimony. Bravely making her way to the front of the church, the smile that Rose's face displayed was one which only the Joy of the Lord could bring. She greeted both Pastor Sonny and Wilson as they directed her towards the front of the congregation. Then she began to speak.

Speaking as loudly as her little voice would carry, Rose shared her testimony beginning with when she was first diagnosed. The place was motionless as people listened to what this woman had to say. Many returned from the night before specifically to hear Rose give her testimony and not a single person was left unmoved. Rose spoke of a time when tears of sadness filled her eyes, and how, now, they had been replaced by tears of joy.

When she arrived at the hospital that morning, everything was in place to proceed with her surgery. However, a few pre-op procedures needed to first be completed. During this time, doctors were bewildered as they were unable to locate the large mass which had been there only days before. Perhaps they had made a mistake? One quick look at Rose's chart and it was unmistakable. For months, doctors watched as this mass continued to grow despite various treatments, and in an instant the Lord had done what the doctors and medicine could not. He had done the impossible! When a mastectomy seemed like the only viable option, God decided He would make His own and this particular option involved the miraculous healing of Rose.

When Rose was finished with her testimony the entire church erupted in praise so loud that it could be heard from miles away. God had performed something amazing here and no one could deny that, least of all Rose.

For I am the Lord your God who takes hold of your right hand and says to you, do not fear; I will help you.

Isaiah 41:13 (NIV)

JESUS HEALS THE SICK WOMAN

When Jesus had again crossed over by boat to the other side of the lake, a large crowd gathered around him while he was by the lake. Then one of the synagogue leaders, named Jairus, came, and when he saw Jesus, he fell at his feet. He pleaded earnestly with him, "My little daughter is dying. Please come and put your hands on her so that she will be healed and live." So Jesus went with him.

A large crowd followed and pressed around him. And a woman was there who had been subject to bleeding for twelve years. She had suffered a great deal under the care of many doctors and had spent all she had, yet instead of getting better she grew worse. When she heard about Jesus, she came up behind him in the crowd and touched his cloak, because she thought, "If I just touch his clothes, I will be healed." Immediately her bleeding stopped and she felt in her body that she was freed from her suffering.

At once Jesus realized that power had gone out from him. He turned around in the crowd and asked, "Who touched my clothes?"

"You see the people crowding against you," his disciples answered, "and yet you can ask, 'Who touched me?'"

But Jesus kept looking around to see who had done it. Then the woman, knowing what had happened to her, came and fell at his feet and, trembling with fear, told him the whole truth. He said to her, "Daughter, your faith has healed you. Go in peace and be freed from your suffering."

Mark 5:21-35 (NIV)

@ POP N' LOCK @

She walked in the side entrance to the gym and took her seat on the bleachers. As she looked out onto the court she saw her son, Caleb, looking back at her. A quick smile on Caleb's face assured her he was glad she came for his game. The players took their positions and with the shrill toot of the referee's whistle the game started.

From the time Caleb could stand he had an affinity for sports. As he grew up that only became stronger. When he was a child there wasn't a day when he wasn't outdoors playing something. He grew up in a family where many of his older brothers and sisters were involved in sports, one even prospected for the minors until sidelined by a knee injury. So, it would be a fair assumption that with all that talent around him, he would be good at one sport at the least. The fact of the matter was, he excelled at many. Baseball, basketball, soccer; you name it. Some of his best childhood memories are those where the family would gather around the TV watching the Knicks at the Garden. Then the next day going outside with his brother and pretending to be those players he admired. By the time he had reached junior high, it was only fitting that he joined the school team.

Even though this was only a scrimmage, Caleb and the other members of his Junior Varsity Basketball team saw this as an opportunity to demonstrate the hours of practice they had put in. And boy did it show! Running up and down the court, proudly sporting their team colors, Caleb and his team started to pull away early in the game and approaching the end of the first half that lead only had grown larger. The team was on cloud nine and Caleb was having a great game. Ostensibly nothing could ruin the momentum.

With the clock running down in the first half, the opposing team kept the ball outside in hopes of narrowing the gap shooting from behind the 3-point line. The ball went up and kissed the rim a few times but never went in. A few more attempts, but the ball could never find its way inside the basket. Now, with inside 30 seconds left in the first half, the opposing team made one last ditch effort to put some more points on the scoreboard. One player threw up a shot which one of Caleb's teammates quickly rebounded. Caleb managed to break away down the court. His teammate passed the ball to him and now it was just him and an open basket. The other team looked on as Caleb ran across the court. Adrenalin now pumping and an open path to the basket, a simple layup seemed inevitable, but this layup was anything but. On a quick approach, Caleb began his ascent to the basket. With all eyes on him, he leaped off the ground and then all pain ensued.

Caleb found himself on the floor just below the opponent's basket, screaming in agony. His teammates ran as fast as they could across the court to get to him. When they arrived, they could hardly believe what they were seeing. The damage was obvious as his left knee cap was now painfully positioned on the side of his leg.

Caleb's mother was already out of her seat and rushing towards him before his body fully came to rest on the hard floor. Together his teammates brought him to the sideline where his coach assessed him. It didn't look good. Once Caleb's mother reached him, she gently placed her hand on Caleb's knee and began to pray. Caleb's coach, Mr. L.F, followed suit by also placing his hands on Caleb's leg, as he agreed with the words that Caleb's mother was speaking. All who were there watched as Caleb's mother and coach prayed over him. And then she said "Amen."

Once Caleb's mother and coach removed their hands, Caleb's knee was healed. His kneecap was sitting exactly where it was meant to, and the agony Caleb was in quickly dissipated. All who were there, especially Caleb, could attest to God's power.

Again, I say unto you, that if two of you shall agree on earth as touching anything that they shall ask, it shall be done for them of My Father which is in heaven.

Matthew 18:19 (KJV)

THE GATE BEAUTIFUL

One day Peter and John were going up to the temple at the time of prayer—at three in the afternoon. Now a man who was lame from birth was being carried to the temple gate called Beautiful, where he was put every day to beg from those going into the temple courts. When he saw Peter and John about to enter, he asked them for money. Peter looked straight at him, as did John. Then Peter said, "Look at us!" So the man gave them his attention, expecting to get something from them.

Then Peter said, "Silver or gold I do not have, but what I do have I give you. In the name of Jesus Christ of Nazareth, walk." Taking him by the right hand, he helped him up, and instantly the man's feet and ankles became strong. He jumped to his feet and began to walk. Then he went with them into the temple courts, walking and jumping, and praising God. When all the people saw him walking and praising God, they recognized him as the same man who used to sit begging at the temple gate called Beautiful, and they were filled with wonder and amazement at what had happened to him.

Acts 3:1-10 (NIV)

ꙮ WART A DAY ꙮ

So often we think we must meet conditions in order for God to act on our behalf. However, we must remember that God's ways are higher than our own and if you believe this to be true, then you must also believe that His concerns are the same. Most people, consciously or not, tend to think that less significant circumstances in our lives, demand less attention from God. Especially when compared to someone whose struggle appears to be far greater. Looking at God, as if He has to choose where to direct His power is one line of thinking that should be adjusted because it makes a difference in how you pray, hope and believe for God's divine intervention in your life. God has unconditional love for you and your circumstances no matter how insignificant you see them in comparison to someone else's. Remember your relationship is between you and your Lord Jesus Christ and as one of His, He desires in

His infinite and ever abounding love to meet your needs. This is something June would learn firsthand.

There June stood, amidst the congregation, with her eyes closed and her hands raised, ever so slightly swaying to the music. There were many things that June could focus on but, as always, she was adamant about this time being reserved for her Lord Jesus Christ. A time set aside not for requests, nor anything other than Praise. As the second song came to an end, June sat in her seat and continued to praise the Lord from her chair. Her eyes remained closed, as she slowly took her seat and rested her hands on her lap for the next two songs. Then she opened her eyes.

It was one quick glance, but that's all it took. June, once again, found her head bowed and with her hands now directed upward, she began to pray.

"Dear God, please, in your infinite power and love, bring healing to my hands. However, I know there are people out there who have to endure much worse than this. So, if you choose not to, I understand. I have already accepted the fact that I might have to live with this and that's ok. I just happened to look down at my hands and thought to present my request one last time. Thank you for your many blessings in my life. In Your holy name – Amen."

It was almost impossible, trying to recall a time when looking at her hands didn't bring up feelings of embarrassment and frustration. Inwardly resigning herself to live with her ailment, consistently trying to reason it from the perspective: *if God wasn't going to miraculously heal my hands, He must have a good reason.* After all, what is a simple case of warts compared to life-threatening diseases such as AIDS or cancer? Perhaps nothing, then again, to God, perhaps everything.

A simple case of warts, however, this certainly was not. For many, simple topical treatments or procedures can usually bring about satisfaction. However, June's condition wasn't so simple. Just like many afflictions, some warts can appear to be an uphill battle and the inconvenience and embarrassment it brings with it can be just as hard to handle.

Being continually ever so conscious of her hands, June was always careful to not let them show in any photos taken of her. Whether it be weddings, birthdays or any other events that required a close-up. For all other times, June simply tried to go about her business giving the matter no thought. This was easier said than done. It is virtually impossible to hide embarrassing overgrown warts on the tops of your hands when you are typing at the computer, signing a check at the bank, not to mention all the other activities that require your hands to be at the center of attention. Even something as simple as joining hands in prayer at church, made for moments filled with apprehension. By this time Google had become her best friend in her quest for a remedy.

After trying myriad naturopathic and over the counter creams, June then tried to freeze them off. After a few weeks of applying the freeze treatment to her warts, things started looking up. The warts turned white and a few days later fell off. This excitement was short lived as they soon began to grow back. That's when she decided that perhaps God would use a doctor to grant her healing. A few promising but painful doctor visits seemed it may do the trick. After various treatments, the doctor suggested cutting them out. Unfortunately, he had to cut well below the actual wart in hopes of removing all the virus responsible. With the warts cut off, June was trying to temper her enthusiasm in case they grew back; and they did. Just two weeks later, not only did the warts grow back, they multiplied.

These pesky warts held their place on top of her hands, as if to taunt her, a constant reminder of a nuisance she couldn't escape. It seemed nothing short of nuking these pesky warts would rid June of them and even then, if a nuclear bomb went off the only two things that would probably survive would be cockroaches and these awful warts! It was about this time that June had resigned herself to living with these things, yet one experience was enough to keep her praying, whether or not she actually believed God would heal her.

Praying in the church one last time for her hands she couldn't help but recall one of the more embarrassing experiences that those troublesome friends which sat upon her hands gave her. Looking to spend the day with her mother, Rebeccah surprised June by bringing them both to get a mani-pedi. Although June committed herself to having a great time with her daughter, she couldn't help noticing the faces the manicurist and others made as they massaged and treated her hands. This was definitely an experience that June wouldn't be forgetting anytime soon.

June left church that day hoping God would hear her last plea, fully expecting that she would have to live with her hands plagued for the rest of her life. She continually tried to come to terms with this annoying condition and knew in her heart she did all she could. Despite various medications, procedures and treatments, and now calling on the name of God, these warts still sat atop her hands. Her feelings shot past hopelessness to complete acquiescence. However, the very next day something truly amazing would happen.

When God intervenes, it always seems as if He waits until the last possible second to act. But nothing is done without reason. In all things to God be the glory and sometimes the way in which our lives work out are to do just that. Give Him glory. After exhausting various homeopathic and over-the-counter remedies, as well as numerous doctor visits, her miracle rested on one last prayer. A prayer to her Lord and Savior Jesus Christ. A prayer that would not return void.

June's eyelids opened just as the sun started making its way over the horizon. This day started out like any other. Before getting out of bed, June laid still for a moment. She prayed for the day and began to arrange in her mind the activities she needed to accomplish. Swinging her legs out from under the covers and down to the floor, she slipped her feet into her slippers. It was an insignificant little itch that drew her attention to her right hand. Now looking down, she noticed something a little out of the ordinary.

Sitting on the end of her bed, now staring at her hands, she noticed that the warts on both her hands had turned a deep brown, almost black color. She remembered her prayer, but June had become accustomed to not getting her hopes up. After all, concerning this issue, she was no stranger to disappointment. It wasn't too long after she first noticed the change in the condition of her warts that they completely fell off. Throughout that day, June couldn't help but think that God had answered the prayer from the day before. It would be two weeks later when her heart would finally be settled on the matter.

With the warts gone for just over two weeks, June caught herself once again looking at her hands. What she saw was healthy unblemished skin which had just about healed over the areas the warts previously occupied. This was when she finally accepted the fact that these warts were healed and weren't coming back. Such a surreal moment of overwhelming joy in that her warts were healed, but more so, that her Lord and Savior Jesus Christ decided to personally take up the matter, when medications, doctors, and various other means had failed.

"Our Jesus hears even the simplest requests, because that's what it was. It popped into my head to try it. I didn't dwell on it like most of my requests. I just asked and God answered."

June Orazi

JESUS HEALS THE TEN MEN

Now on his way to Jerusalem, Jesus traveled along the border between Samaria and Galilee. As he was going into a village, ten men who had leprosy met him. They stood at a distance and called out in a loud voice, "Jesus, Master, have pity on us!"

When he saw them, he said, "Go, and show yourselves to the priests." And as they went, they were cleansed.

One of them, when he saw he was healed, came back, praising God in a loud voice. He threw himself at Jesus' feet and thanked him—and he was a Samaritan.

Jesus asked, "Were not all ten cleansed? Where are the other nine? Has no one returned to give praise to God except this foreigner?" Then he said to him, "Rise and go; your faith has made you well."

Luke 17:11-19 (NIV)

ɷ YOU'VE GOT ME IN STITCHES ɷ

Haiti is an extremely dangerous and spiritually active place. It is a place where God has been cast out and the country has been dedicated to Satan. A place where kidnapping and murder are a daily occurrence, only to be outdone by the amount of voodoo worship. It is a place where evil spirits seem comfortable enough to manifest themselves and freely roam the country. Combine a corrupt government, extreme poverty, and the enslavement of Haitians by their neighbors in the Dominican Republic, as well as among their own people, and you have the makings for an extremely volatile place. For this reason, one must be absolutely certain that God has called them before starting a ministry in Haiti. The last place to be, is a place like Haiti, outside the perfect will of God. It is for this reason Liz spent weeks in prayer before finally deciding to go.

It was her first trip to Haiti and the most memorable. Stepping foot on Haitian soil was an experience like none other. Not to say she wasn't anxious, but notwithstanding the incredibly hostile climate of the country she knew with all her heart she was there for a purpose. The ride to where they were staying was just the beginning of her experiences. When we think of our living situation in the States, we think of wealthy, middle class working, and low-income neighborhoods. In Haiti, Liz was amazed to discover, that on any particular street there could be a walled off mansion protected by guards with machine guns and the very next lot would be a house, if you could call it that, with a tin roof which used to be one of the walls of a truck. This whole trip would be an eye-opening experience on many different levels, however let's start at the beginning.

From early on, Liz knew she had a special calling on her life, however she didn't know exactly what it was. So, when opportunity to join a well-known organization in the mission field was made available, she strongly considered it. Their destination this time was Haiti. No one from the family had ever been to Haiti, but after much prayer Liz decided to go. What made it a little easier was that her uncle James would also be joining her.

The primary mission on this trip was twofold. Preaching the gospel of Jesus Christ and building houses for those in need. This was a trip assembled with the intentions of helping others and becoming closer to Christ. By the end, all intentions were more than met. Liz learned from this trip that sometimes we must experience less than ideal circumstances in order for God to show His glory and bring us closer to Him.

They greatly anticipated this trip but were made very aware that their visit would be falling on one of the major Voodoo high holy weeks. A time set aside each year to commemorate the dedication of the country to Satan. It is a time when the extremely unpredictable climate of the country becomes even more so. And yet, it was a time that God had set aside for Liz to do His work and experience Him like never before.

It had been three days since Liz's arrival to Haiti and other than a miserable first night, due to her over awareness of the possibility of a four-inch tarantula climbing into her bed, everything was going great. For the last two days Liz had been involved in building houses with the other members of her team and things were progressing quicker than anticipated. She also involved herself in the clothing and food ministries.

It was the morning of the fourth day, Liz woke up and couldn't wait to get started. All reservations she previously had about this trip had since vanished. She quickly got herself ready as not to keep the rest of her team waiting before they left for that day's assignment. Preparing to leave, she opened the door to her room and what awaited her just on the other side was enough to make anyone rethink their decision to come.

There it hung, outside her room door, tied to her doorknob swinging, in an unblinking stare. A horrific smell unlike anything she had ever experienced. A river of blood flowing across the path in which she would have to walk to get out of her room. It seemed every fly gravitated to this one spot outside her door where the devil himself could almost be heard taunting her, trying to make her question her decision to make this trip. What hung there as she opened the door to her room was the rotting severed head of a fully-grown cow and from the smell of it, one that had been dead for some time. Liz was quickly able to put it into perspective. Still, it was a sober reminder that this wasn't someplace to let your guard down. A reminder that 'she wasn't in Kansas anymore'; I mean New York.

A severed cow head tied to the outside of one's door seems intense enough, but for Liz, this was just the beginning of a thirty-day trip which seemed to be plagued with unfortunate events. These ranged from having all her clothing stolen to near death experiences. One of the more memorable being the time she was almost crushed to death.

It couldn't have been more than two weeks into her trip when the leader told Liz and her group that they would be assigned to a new building project. This project involved building seminary dormitories. Once on location Liz and the other members of the team got right to work. The plan was to start with the outer walls and work inward.

One by one the team members hauled the heavy cinderblocks to the location where the wall was being built. From there they were staggered one on top of another with a thin set of mortar in-between. With the wall now approaching five feet the members focused their attention towards building the adjacent wall. Once again, one by one the blocks were stacked and mortared. Liz having just returned with a block, set out to grab another from the pile. On her way back, she heard someone yelling but paid it no mind. So, she continued to walk. Then she heard the yelling once again. This time she couldn't help but notice the extreme distress in the voice of the person yelling. So, she turned to find the five-foot wall that she helped build was now falling towards her. Every instinct in her screamed for her to move, but all she could do was stand there paralyzed and watch as the wall tipped closer and closer. All watched in horror as the wall fell. Surely, she was dead. After all, who could survive getting crushed by over 1,000 pounds of cinderblock?

The event happened so quickly but what Liz remembers is closing her eyes as the wall was about to hit her. The wall slammed against the floor sending a thick cloud of debris and dirt into the area. All those present ran over hoping for the best but expecting the very worst.

Once the dust settled everyone looked on in amazement. Liz looked down at her feet and noticed the wall landed only inches from her toes. If this wasn't divine protection what was? God still had one more thing to show her. One more event on this trip which would solidify her belief that God is her Abba Father.

With only a week remaining and the building projects winding down, the members of the group had more personal time. They now had the opportunity to explore the people and the country more intimately. A chance to learn more about this place where God had brought them.

After finishing up a few final items on the building checklist, the group decided, since it was still very early, they would take a walk and explore the surrounding area. One thing that never ceased to amaze everyone was the massive amount of rubble and garbage everywhere. Such a vast amount that any attempt to clean it would be futile. With each passing day and every new observation, Liz became more appreciative of her life and the blessings she didn't thank God enough for. To this day, not a morning goes by where Liz doesn't come to God, thanking Him for every provision in her life. Especially when she looks down at her leg and sees the faded scar, a reminder of one particular event from this trip. One of the many in her life that keep her staunch in her belief that God cares for His children. That God cares for her.

It wasn't a very long walk but it was long enough to give Liz time to ponder a question that kept entering her mind throughout this trip. Having never had the time to thoroughly examine it, she looked around as she walked. She noticed the people, their living conditions and their struggles. Then she found the answer to her question. God seems to move in miraculous ways on behalf of the people here because they have nothing else. It's only them and God.

"When we feel ill, we run to our medicine cabinet. When we are hungry, we go to the cupboard or refrigerator. When we feel threatened, we call the police and when we meet life changing injuries or diagnosis, we go to the hospital. These are all luxuries or shall I say blessings from God that the people of Haiti are not familiar with. Examining God's people in Haiti brought an amazing awareness of how little we rely on God at home."

It was one careless misstep but that's all it took to send Liz to the ground in pain tightly gripping her lower leg. The other members of the group immediately surrounded her as one reached into a bag and pulled out a little First Aid kit. Gently washing away the blood from the wound, they quickly assessed the damage. To everyone's horror, on the back of Liz's leg was a deep 3-inch laceration. Despite everyone's best efforts, the bleeding wouldn't stop. One member looked over and acknowledged the sharp piece of metal, which was most likely the culprit for the injury. Because of the extreme filth and high probability of infection, all strongly urged Liz to go to the hospital. Yet, whether sensible or not, the one thing Liz feared more than possible infection was the prospect of going to a Haitian hospital.

After some arguing, Liz agreed to go to the hospital if things didn't appear to be better by morning. With two butterfly bandages they managed to pull the wound closed and with one person under each arm, they helped Liz walk back to where they were staying. Once back, all gathered around and prayed that God would miraculously heal their friend and with every word prayed, Liz fervently hoped that God would answer.

Liz spent the night tossing and turning, trying to get the thoughts of having to go to the hospital in the morning out of her head. She fully believed that God could do a miracle, but never really expected God to show up in her time of need. It's always for someone else, somewhere else and yet, she prayed to God until roughly 2:00 a.m. when sleep finally overcame her.

As the sun began to clear away the night, Liz's eyelids started to open. It was still very early and she was still half conscious from the few hours of sleep she had gotten. In her semi-conscious state she started scratching her leg. Quickly becoming aware of what she was doing, she panicked and pulled the covers off of her. It was certain, given the extent of her injury, that any progress the wound made healing overnight was undone when she scratched. Fully expecting to see blood pouring from the wound, she instead stared dumbfounded.

Closer examination exhibited the skills of an experienced surgeon. One who mended the wound with a purposeful hand. A testimony Liz would forever carry with her about a time when God miraculously healed her leg. A time when God, yet again, showed His love.

"God's favor in your life is where His perfect will is for you. Ask God to reveal His purpose for you, walk in it, and just watch what He will do."

Elizabeth Snow

JESUS HEALS THE CRIPPLED WOMAN

On a Sabbath Jesus was teaching in one of the synagogues, and a woman was there who had been crippled by a spirit for eighteen years. She was bent over and could not straighten up at all. When Jesus saw her, he called her forward and said to her, "Woman, you are set free from your infirmity." Then he put his hands on her, and immediately she straightened up and praised God.

Indignant because Jesus had healed on the Sabbath, the synagogue leader said to the people, "There are six days for work. So come and be healed on those days, not on the Sabbath."

The Lord answered him, "You hypocrites! Doesn't each of you on the Sabbath untie your ox or donkey from the stall and lead it out to give it water? Then should not this woman, a daughter of Abraham, whom Satan has kept bound for eighteen long years, be set free on the Sabbath day from what bound her?"

When he said this, all his opponents were humiliated, but the people were delighted with all the wonderful things he was doing.

Luke 13:10-17 (NIV)

ω NEED A LIFT ω

Moving his hand quickly, he managed to grasp the bottom corner of his list before it blew out the window of his car. It started out a pretty uneventful day, but by day's end John's mind wouldn't be able to focus on anything else. Understandably, when God intervenes on someone's behalf, how could anyone's focus be elsewhere? Here of all places, why? It didn't seem the ideal backdrop for a movement of God's power and yet, there it was. It wasn't while praying, during any benevolent act, neither during any other situation that would assume the Lord's favor. That's it! There are no prerequisites in order for the Lord to act on your behalf. There is no such thing as the perfect setting, situation, or set of circumstances. The perfect time is whenever the Lord acts, and it is always perfect.

When our time comes and we go to our final home that Jesus has prepared for us, what will we know? Without getting too philosophical, the question that I'm getting at is this: is there going to be a point when we can suddenly look over the course of our lives and see every moment God intervened on our behalf? Just think about it for a second. Most would see your car running out of gas as an unfortunate event. But what if God let that happen in order for you to avoid a serious accident that resulted in your passing. This is just something to think about.

It's easy to say that God intervenes continuously in our lives, but it's another thing to believe. That's one of the reasons why I believe that, rather than positioning certain events to work out in our favor, God sometimes has to do, what we would label, an outright miracle. Something we cannot write off as a close call, happenstance or even luck (as if there were such a thing), truly a miraculous event in which we have no other choice but to acknowledge that God is taking ever constant notice of our lives. On one particular afternoon, this would become something of which John would be only too aware.

It wasn't too pressing of a day, just running a few errands and perhaps stopping to meet with friends. If there was ever a beautiful day on Long Island it was this day. Sunny and 70. Perfect for driving with the windows down and the radio on. It didn't take long before John had finished doing the last on his list. It was still early afternoon, so it was off to meet up with friends. Just one quick stop home first.

Making the turn onto Hallock Landing Road, he made his way back toward home. Traffic was light. Much of the way comprised of a long stretch of evergreens lining both sides of what seemed like an endless road. In reality it was only a few miles. But it would be on these few miles that John would have yet another moment where God would show up in a miraculous way.

There is nothing like when you're driving with the windows rolled down belting out your favorite tunes because your favorite song came on the radio. Looking at the tree shaped air freshener, giving your old car that faint new car smell, dancing on that little string hanging from the rear view mirror. It can make a monotonous trip, if only for a few minutes, a little less so.

There John was, driving down the road without a care in the world and in an instant, he found himself gripping the steering wheel. With his heart racing and anxiety through the roof, processing all the thoughts now flooding his mind was nearly impossible. Quickly finding a place on the side of the road, he maneuvered his car to its resting place.

Only a few seconds earlier, without any warning, three small children and their pet darted across the road only a few yards in front of his car. With little chance of maneuvering the car in time, there was little John could do.

There was no mistaking the loud thump that he heard! With the thump still echoing in his head and the immediate drop of his heart into his stomach, it was all John could do to keep from seeing what he ate for lunch. The worst case scenarios started circling in his mind and even though there was no denying he hit something, his only prayer was that it wasn't one of the children.

It was no more than 15 seconds and John was already pulled off against the side of the road and jumping out of his car. He quickly ran out into the road where he fully expected to be greeted by the unimaginable. The sight of an injured or possibly dead child. Running towards the middle of the road, in a complete panic, he looked everywhere, but to his surprise could find no injured victims.

He clearly saw the children and there was no denying the loud thump. However, as he looked around he found no evidence of anything having been hit. In fact, there was no evidence of any children. Just as John slowed his sprint in the middle of the road another car came barreling down the road and struck him from behind.

What caused the driver of the other vehicle to avert his attention from the road will probably never be known. The smell of burned rubber filled the air. Leaving a black cloud trailing behind, the tires screeched as they tried to grip the cracked asphalt. Then the car came to a stop.

Most would avoid even the thought of themselves or a loved one being hit by a car. Even more so, one which involves being struck from behind at over 60 mph. -The unexpected impact instantly crushing the lower spine, continues its ongoing assault by running over the victim. The hot rubber from the tires and the steel undercarriage remain steadfast in its brutal demolition of the already broken body, which seemed to be lifelessly dragged against the pavement for a while before eventually coming free. At which time rolling another few yards before all momentum is lost and the lifeless body finally comes to rest.- A very tangible reality for anyone in a similar situation to John this day. However, God had another reality for John.

It took about fifty feet, but the car finally screeched its way to a halt. To only imagine what the driver of the vehicle must have been thinking as he looked through his windshield. A day starting with the normalcy of any other now culminated to this very moment where there are just no words to describe the silence that followed soon after.

When I was just a child, I believed that whenever a random moment of silence transpired, an angel was present. Perhaps there is more to this than just superstition.

There John sat, on the end of the car completely frozen, trying to process all that had just transpired. With one deep breath his trivial stare on the road ahead of him was broken. Sliding off the front end of the car, he couldn't help but notice the areas on the backs of his upper legs which were now extremely sore. It took over ten minutes sitting in his car on the side of the road, but with his heart rate finally normalizing and adrenaline wearing off, he took his car out of park and made his way home.

Entering his home, his mother immediately read the look on his face. But before she could ask anything, John started to tell of the amazing events that had taken place. He spoke of seeing the children and dog darting out in front of his car and how he was sure he hit one of them. He then spoke of getting hit by a car. A story almost unbelievable to himself had he not been the one involved. As he proceeded through his experience his mother knew this was no ordinary story. Furthering along his account he now told of the car striking him from behind.

Almost every possible scenario had the story playing out with significant injury. The first and most probable was that when the car ran over John he would end up under the car. Scenario two, would have John rolling up the top of the car and hitting the windshield before either flipping completely over the car or rolling back off the front as the car came to an abrupt stop. Then there is the last possible scenario. Number three. God's.

The car came to an abrupt stop, and there John sat on the front end of the car as if he were placed there. In fact, that's exactly what happened. He told his mother that day of the most amazing experience. Something that would never be forgotten. As the car struck John, he felt what could only be described as a pair of hands lifting him. There was no doubting something supernatural had happened. No doubt that God sent an angel to protect him in his time of need. The angel lifted him, placed him on the hood of that car and held him steady in a seated position until the car came to its stop. Following his story, he showed his mother the two rose and purple areas on the backs of his legs. Clearly noticeable, his mother acknowledged the two bruises and thanked God for protecting her son.

PAUL AND SILAS IN PRISON

Once when we were going to the place of prayer, we were met by a female slave who had a spirit by which she predicted the future. She earned a great deal of money for her owners by fortune-telling. She followed Paul and the rest of us, shouting, "These men are servants of the Most High God, who are telling you the way to be saved." She kept this up for many days. Finally Paul became so annoyed that he turned around and said to the spirit, "In the name of Jesus Christ I command you to come out of her!" At that moment the spirit left her.

When her owners realized that their hope of making money was gone, they seized Paul and Silas and dragged them into the marketplace to face the authorities. They brought them before the magistrates and said, "These men are Jews, and are throwing our city into an uproar by advocating customs unlawful for us Romans to accept or practice."

The crowd joined in the attack against Paul and Silas, and the magistrates ordered them to be stripped and beaten with rods. After they had been severely flogged, they were thrown into prison, and the jailer was commanded to guard them carefully. When he received these orders, he put them in the inner cell and fastened their feet in the stocks.

About midnight Paul and Silas were praying and singing hymns to God, and the other prisoners were listening to them. Suddenly there was such a violent earthquake that the foundations of the prison were shaken. At once all the prison doors flew open, and everyone's chains came loose. The jailer woke up, and when he saw the prison doors open, he drew his sword and was about to kill himself because he thought the prisoners had escaped. But Paul shouted, "Don't harm yourself! We are all here!"

The jailer called for lights, rushed in and fell trembling before Paul and Silas. He then brought them out and asked, "Sirs, what must I do to be saved?"

They replied, "Believe in the Lord Jesus, and you will be saved—you and your household." Then they spoke the word of the Lord to him and to all the others in his house. At that hour of the night the jailer took them and washed their wounds; then immediately he and all his household were baptized. The jailer brought them into his house and set a meal before them; he was filled with joy because he had come to believe in God—he and his whole household.

When it was daylight, the magistrates sent their officers to the jailer with the order: "Release those men." The jailer told Paul, "The magistrates have ordered that you and Silas be released. Now you can leave. Go in peace."

But Paul said to the officers: "They beat us publicly without a trial, even though we are Roman citizens, and threw us into prison. And now do they want to get rid of us quietly? No! Let them come themselves and escort us out."

The officers reported this to the magistrates, and when they heard that Paul and Silas were Roman citizens, they were alarmed. They came to appease them and escorted them from the prison, requesting them to leave the city. After Paul and Silas came out of the prison, they went to Lydia's house, where they met with the brothers and sisters and encouraged them. Then they left.

Acts 16: 16-40 (NIV)

ⓠ THE LOGICAL WATER SOLUTION ⓠ

It started with a few drops hitting against the window pane. With eyes agape, Ryan slowly followed one of the water drops down its path across the surface of the window. Trying to predict which path it would take was no simple task. Once the drop ran below the window, he then drew his attention to another. The sound of rain hitting the roof accelerated and there was no mistaking, it was now pouring. Leaning back in his chair he continued to stare out the window. He watched the tree at the edge of the street swaying in the wind. A mindless distraction taking his attention from the work he needed to accomplish. Clearly his mind was elsewhere and his boss noticed.

The soft tap of a co-worker's hand on his left shoulder pulled him from his daze back into reality. "Walter would like to see you," she said, swiftly passing by on her way to the building's exit. Ryan quickly assembled his papers and made his way towards Walter's office. Walking in the office door that was left ajar, Ryan gave a brief knock and made his presence known.

"Walter, you wanted to see me? "

"Yeah, Ryan, have a seat."

A pretty informal office, very casual and friendly. A place where co-workers were treated more like family than work associates. Pouring coffee into his black and blue ceramic mug, Walter said, "There is plenty of coffee if you would like some, just help yourself. There's also some donuts on the desk over there." Now, both with coffee in hand, Walter's reason for Ryan's call to the office was made known.

Sitting across the table from each other, Walter said. "You wish you were back?" with a subtle empathic expression on his face.

"It's that obvious, huh?"

"Mhmm," Walter replied.

"There's just something about that place. Something about the people. I just can't explain it."

One Year Earlier

It was sort of a compelling feeling, as if something was urging him to make a decision. There was no doubting what it was. Ryan's parents had been in ministry for some time and as he sat in the sanctuary of his father's church he felt a stirring. Today's guest speaker was a man from (Organization's name withheld).

Ryan listened attentively, as story after story was told of how God was using this ministry to further His cause. The man mentioned that God was leading their ministry to revisit Mexico City. Just when Ryan thought that compelling feeling couldn't get any stronger, he was proven wrong. As the man continued to engage the congregation with the work being done in Mexico, Ryan couldn't help but feel drawn to this place.

A few days had passed and Ryan still couldn't shake that feeling. The one he had felt so strongly sitting amidst the congregation that previous Sunday. So, in an effort to receive sound advice he consulted his mother.

It wasn't a lengthy conversation, but as Ryan and his mother sat at the kitchen table, it became quickly apparent that a decision would have to be made. That afternoon, his mother would confirm what he already knew. That the compelling feeling which plagued him the last few days, was that of the Lord trying to get his attention. Without any reservations, Ryan's mother agreed that God was calling him to the mission field and that he should consider this upcoming opportunity and so he did.

Finding yourself in the will of God is truly a feeling that not even the best vocabulary can do justice. But the phrase I'll use is "simply amazing" and this is something Ryan discovered immediately. The smell in the air, the sight of the red tint to the clay dirt and the warmth from the hot Mexican sun all seemed to speak in unison as if to acknowledge a God ordained reason for being there. From every confirmation, to every open door, Ryan continued to walk forward in pursuit of this calling. Now standing amidst the people of this country, he discovered a deeper and more personal understanding of God's heart for His creation. With an undeterred focus, Ryan found that amidst hopelessness, extreme poverty and life's uncertainty, God's grace and ever abounding love seemed to be more tangible than at any other point in his life.

The few weeks that Ryan spent in Mexico were life changing. A completely humbling experience feeding and bringing moments of happiness into the lives of thousands of people. A time of being at perfect peace, demonstrating the love and character of Christ to all those God placed in his path. One where the distractions and business of life, seemed to take a back seat to true purpose. Being about the business of Christ...

"Unfulfilling."

Ryan responded, "That word couldn't be any more perfect, that's exactly what I've been feeling. Unfulfilled."

The room went silent for a moment. Ryan looked across the table and it was obvious, from the look on his face, that Walter was pondering something. Perhaps a little bit of an inner struggle whether or not to say what he had on his mind. But clearly this meeting was God ordained, because what he said next would be the one thing that would put Ryan back in the mission field. Sitting across from Ryan was a man who, although he didn't know Christ at this time, saw Christ's purpose in Ryan's life and was used by the Lord to propel him back into the perfect will of God.

"As much as I hate to lose you here, I believe that you need to go back to Mexico. You will have a place here should you decide to return but, for now, you need to follow your true purpose."

Only a few months later Ryan found himself going through déjà vu, boarding another Mexico bound flight. June 1996 would mark the beginning of a six-month mission trip, in which he would experience God's intervention unlike anything he had ever dreamt possible.

He was only a few steps outside the airport and already the word "unfulfilled" was lost from his vocabulary.

The emptiness that afflicted his heart completely evaporated once he returned his feet to Mexico's clayed earth.

Colonias de Coyote

We often hear of being humbled, but seldom dive deeper into the process of that which is learned from the humbling experience. In fact, this experience as a whole encompasses a lot more revelation than generically assumed.

It was a small community, not even sure it could constitute a village, but it was known as El Colonias de Coyote or Colony of the coyote. It was here where a kind family would open up their home and provide a place for Ryan to stay during his time in Mexico. With little more than 200 square feet, complete with a dirt floor, this family welcomed a perfect stranger into their home and their hospitality was rivaled by none. Finding humility amongst his new family was very easy. What little they had they would offer freely and in everything gave thanks. It was impossible to ignore that these people possessed something innate. A trait too seldom seen back in the States. What was it? It was Joy. In everything they had, or lack thereof, they gave thanks. It was in this that Ryan started to examine further what God was trying to show him. Through this process of humility, Ryan began to understand the extreme demonstration of God's love through others, despite grim circumstances. In addition, he discovered more about the potential the Holy Spirit placed in him, to endure hardship and demonstrate that same love to others. Yet, above learning about himself and others, Ryan found that this process opened a connection with God he had never previously experienced. A place where he could feel the heart of God. A line of communication that couldn't easily be severed.

Side Walk Sunday School (SWSS)

During this second trip, Ryan was a member of one of four teams that were sent out, whose ministry was primarily directed towards children. This multifaceted ministry had two primary focuses and left such a lasting impression, that Ryan would later duplicate the ministry back in the States.

The first was through its ministry known as 'Side Walk Sunday School' (SWSS). It was a ministry in which Sunday school was brought to children in the streets of Mexico City. A place where families could gather with their children and experience the word of God through puppet shows, songs, and interactive games. This was an experience that children and their parents looked forward to. A place where along the dusty streets of Mexico City, the Joy of the Lord would become present. A moment in which families could break away from life's mundane routine and learn about their loving Savior.

The second part of this ministry, which followed SWSS, involved an extremely large feeding program. In addition to feeding upwards of 30,000 children a month through 'Side Walk Sunday School', thousands of families who normally would have gone hungry also went to bed with full bellies.

There were too many heartfelt moments that inspired tears within this ministry. Whether it was a hug from a child who hadn't eaten in days or a grateful smile from his mother who couldn't find the words to say. All emotions seemed to well up from deep within, as if to give a taste of the heart of God for those He loves.

Holy Water

There were countless moments where God divinely intervened throughout Ryan's stay in Mexico. But one particular moment stood apart from the rest. It's such an amazing thing how God can orchestrate circumstances and people in our lives to accomplish what would seem almost impossible otherwise. Although, this defined as a miracle isn't any less significant, there is something that stands out when God Himself intervenes through unnatural, better yet supernatural means.

They were nearly finished setting up and already hundreds were waiting for them to begin. To say it was unusually hot would be an understatement, but all were in good spirits. Throughout SWSS, children and families were given bottles of water to ward off the overbearing heat from the day's oppressive sun. It was an obvious observation that the ministry was going through more supplies than normal, but they had anticipated and stocked accordingly. Or so they thought.

As SWSS came to an end, other members of the team began setting up for the food ministry. The immediate concern loomed as to whether or not enough provisions were brought to feed all who came. What started out as a couple hundred people had ballooned to almost three times that. Indeed, God would have to perform a Matthew 14 miracle.

As one vehicle after another was emptied of their supplies, the concern became even more heart wrenching that some people might have to leave without. The real possibility some children came with the hopes of eating, perhaps their first meal in days, and would be turned away because of lack of provisions. However, God did the impossible. With the last family given food and water, what was left of the supplies was just enough to hydrate ministry members. So each member, including Ryan was given a bottle of water and began to help disassemble and pack up the trucks.

Stepping away for a moment, Ryan took a few minutes to himself before returning to help disassemble.

Every day was extremely fulfilling, nonetheless exhausting. From the moment ministry members started to set up to the time the last family was fed, there was not a moment's rest. Moreover, the heat seemed to zap the energy from one while just standing. However, the main reason Ryan would take some time alone every day, was to try to hear from the Lord.

During the minutes he took for himself this day, a small boy came up to him. From his chapped lips and bushed look, it was obvious that this child was in need of some water. So without hesitation Ryan gave his last bottle of water to this child. Ryan noticed the look on the child's face when given the water. It was the same look a child gets when they open up their gifts on Christmas. Grateful and with a quick smile the boy walked away drinking. Ryan smiled as he walked back towards the trucks. "There's nothing more fulfilling."

Higher Quality H2O

It couldn't have been more than an hour later. His headache started as a little annoyance but quickly grew to something unbearable. Ryan did everything he could to put the pain out of his mind but the more he tried to not think about it, the worse it seemed to become. It was clear by this point that Ryan had become dehydrated and unfortunately he had given his very last bottle away.

Ryan found himself alongside the road where he listened for God's voice earlier. However this time, it was merely to rest from the weariness that plagued him. It wasn't a long drawn out prayer, but a simple request. With both his hands pressed against the sides of his head, Ryan said, "God, please help my head."

Turning to head back towards the trucks, which were nearly packed up, he noticed a short old lady standing next to him. This peculiar old lady couldn't have been more than 5' but what Ryan couldn't take his eyes off of, was her smile. Without a word, she raised her right hand towards him revealing a plastic bottle filled with water. There was something unusual about this bottle but he couldn't quite put his finger on it. Nearly overwhelmed at the kind gesture, Ryan took the water bottle and replied, "Muchas gracias." The second that bottle hit his hand he realized what puzzled him about it. There was condensation on it and it was extremely cold. "How is it… where would someone… it's not possible." Yet, all that mattered now was, through this lady's kind gesture, Ryan had water. He first ran the bottle across his forehead in an effort to dull some of the pain, followed by opening the bottle and drinking.

For over fifteen years Ryan has been on a crusade of sorts, in an effort to bring the highest quality water to, not only Florida residents but other states as well. It has been fifteen years of diligently searching for more efficient and proficient ways of purifying one of God's most valued resources. It was truly a revelation to think back and discover this passion was all inspired by a simple bottle of water. And yet that bottle wasn't so simple, after all.

The first drops that hit his tongue spelt instant hydration and as those drops became a pour, his headache began to subside until it was completely gone. What kind of water was this? It was without a doubt water, but there was something about it that screamed extraordinary. With his head tilted back, Ryan consumed the whole bottle. He quickly noted the feeling of his body being revitalized as the water made its way through. Ounce after ounce was more enlivening than the last. Once finished he looked down to once again thank the old lady, but to his amazement she was gone. He quickly looked for her in every direction but there was no sign of her. The landscape was open for at least fifteen-yards in all directions, so there was little chance that this little old lady was hidden. After a moment or two, Ryan chuckled to himself and remembered his prayer from earlier. With a believing disbelief over what he had just experienced, he gave thanks to the Lord.

Checkmate

"Checkmate!" Ryan exclaimed, as his younger brother Daniel was forced to tip his king and concede victory for the third game in a row. It was a nice handcrafted marble black and white chess set, that Ryan could barely wait to present him. It was during these chess games that Ryan shared with Daniel all the experiences he had and all the amazing things that God had shown him over the last six months. He shared one amazing story after another. But the one that stuck out the most, was the story about when God decided to send an angel with one amazing bottle of water. A bottle of water so perfect to the taste and a texture so divine, it had to be from heaven itself.

"He'll not only get you through situations, God's grace will allow you to do so triumphantly."

-Ryan Confusione

JESUS FEEDS THE FIVE THOUSAND

When Jesus heard what had happened, he withdrew by boat privately to a solitary place. Hearing of this, the crowds followed him on foot from the towns. When Jesus landed and saw a large crowd, he had compassion on them and healed their sick.

As evening approached, the disciples came to him and said, "This is a remote place, and it's already getting late. Send the crowds away, so they can go to the villages and buy themselves some food."

Jesus replied, "They do not need to go away. You give them something to eat."

"We have here only five loaves of bread and two fish," they answered.

"Bring them here to me," he said. And he directed the people to sit down on the grass. Taking the five loaves and the two fish and looking up to heaven, he gave thanks and broke the loaves. Then he gave them to the disciples, and the disciples gave them to the people. They all ate and were satisfied, and the disciples picked up twelve basketfuls of broken pieces that were left over. The number of those who ate was about five thousand men, besides women and children.

Matthew 14:13-21 (NIV)

ꝏ PRAYER ꝏ

Ideally, the impression of prayer to most is a pretty positive one. But how many really take the time to try to understand it further? Do we merely use prayer as a good gesture telling someone "I'll keep you in prayer," never to give that person another thought, let alone actually pray? Has praying become so routine that God's sovereign power and ability to miraculously answer is overlooked? Or do we float in another category where our view of praying is much like throwing spaghetti against the wall hoping some will stick. Committing ourselves to prayer, knowing its potential, but never really believing God will answer.

Prayer happens to be the most important and most valuable tool God gives us. It is, in its simplest definition, our line of communication with our Heavenly Father and that's not to be taken blithely. Praying is not just intercession with our Lord but an act of faith. One only needs to read Matthew 17:20 to see the potential that the smallest measure of faith can have. Prayer is an amazing thing because its inherent nature is that of our Lord and Savior Jesus Christ. Prayers, just like our Heavenly Father, are boundless. There is no distance too far, no obstacle too big that can keep God from hearing them. They can even transcend time and space. It is out of love most prayers are born, and out of love God answers.

So next time you're in need, Give it a try! You might just be surprised.

ℚ SAVING GRACE ℚ

One of the greatest experiences that any blood bought believer in Christ can have, is to enter into the presence of the Lord. It is an experience that transcends everything else. A moment where all the cares of life seem to be forgotten in an unbelievable moment of amazing harmony with your Redeemer.

It was a closeness, sense of security, friendship and, most of all, an all-encompassing, awe-inspiring, flawless tangible feeling of the Lord's amazing love amidst one of the biggest trials of her life. When death seemed to be looming, as its friend 'fear' looked to wreak havoc on her mind, her Lord came and rescued her.

There were more than seventy people. The house was certainly snug, however large enough to accommodate all. It was a different time, perhaps one that we will revisit soon, where regardless of denomination and differences, people came together under one roof in the unity of Christ. They were called house meetings and this Wednesday evening, many came from different churches to this home where they looked forward to listening to a man, by the name of Kumar, speak. He was a pastor who Loaves and Fishes Ministries had supported for some time. A person who was outspoken about his faith, amongst the persecution of Christians in India. He was a man of God, a prophet filled with the Holy Spirit and what he would speak this evening would forever be singed in the heart and mind of one particular individual. It would be the beginning of an amazing testimony that she would boldly speak of years later. A miracle that would serve as a living demonstration offering the Lord's peace and security to many women who would have to endure the same.

The Prophecy

Her efforts to weave through the crowd, close enough to discover who was getting prayed over, were fruitless. However, Tish listened closely as Pastor Kumar's prophecy from the Lord went forth. It was a lengthy word which spoke of someone who would go through a very devastating time. A time of extreme testing, where fear would look to take hold and death would be waiting. But who was it? As the prophecy went forth, it seemed complete misery was destined for the one getting prayed over and that nothing short of the Lord's grace would be able to preserve. The crowd listened quietly as the words spoken went from bad to worse. But the congregation began to praise the Lord as the last part of the prophecy was spoken. A promise that the Lord would never leave or forsake.

Once the service came to an end, the crowd started to disperse and Tish was finally able to advance towards the front of the house. Her sister, Fran and her husband Pastor Sonny were that evening's hosts. They had graciously opened up their home to the Pastor and all those who wished to hear him speak. Absolutely no one left that home without being touched. She finally made it up to the front of the house and with her curiosity piqued she said to her sister, "I wonder who that was for?"

With a smile and a slight chuckle, Fran turned and said, "It was for me."

One moment she was agreeing in prayer and the next she was the one getting prayed over. With her eyes closed and head bowed, Fran was surprised to feel a pair of hands laid upon her head. Then, the Pastor began prophesying over her. Fran was unsure of how to feel towards these words exiting the pastor's mouth. Yet, in spite of how grim that prophecy began, Fran to this day, finds her true love letter from the Lord in how it ended. Those last words that Pastor Kumar spoke would forever be sealed upon Fran's heart and would be those words that Fran would cling to amidst her trial. A promise directly from God that He would be the one to help her rise above, on eagle's wings, what she would soon have to face. These words were, "Grace, Grace and more Grace. You will be comforted in the fellowship of His suffering."

It All Started with a Little Girl

It was over a year later that Fran found herself traveling down a familiar backroad of her hometown. The memory of the prophecy spoken by Pastor Kumar, by this time, had become an occasional remembrance. Something thought about in passing but never dwelled upon. It came out of nowhere but as she was driving she felt the sudden urge to adopt another child. She knew instantly that it was the Lord. So, she asked, "Lord, why are you putting it in my heart to have another child?"

As clear as day, the Lord responded, "As a baby she will not be beautiful as others regard beauty, but you will love her." She did grow up to be a beautiful young woman. But as an infant, this couldn't have been truer.

It was a small ad in a local magazine known as the 'Penny Saver'. A few weeks had passed since she heard God speak to her and now Fran found herself reading a small advertisement from a woman who was facilitating adoptions in Romania. It was a new era in the country's history. With the overthrown communist regime and the death of the

Ceausescu, the adoption of Romanian children was now possible. A magazine ordinarily destined for the top of the junk drawer was used by God to further direct Fran and confirm what she'd heard the Lord speak.

Telling him of the article, Fran said to her husband, "I think God wants us to adopt from Romania. I saw an article about an information meeting in the Penny Saver, let's go."

Sonny responded, "We don't have the money for that." But Fran assured him that just as God had made provision in all their previous adoptions, God would provide. And so God did.

They went to the adoption meeting. It was Thanksgiving week in the autumn of 1990. Fran and Sonny found themselves in a familiar place once again filling out reams of paperwork and getting fingerprinted. It was only two weeks later when Fran was given a message that the adoption facilitator, whose name was also Fran, had called and wished an immediate call back. Did I mess up the paperwork? Will we have to start all over? Are we denied the adoption? Every negative thought flooded her mind as she prepared to return the call. Their paperwork had only been in Romania for two weeks and now Fran listened in amazement as the adoption facilitator asked, "How would you like an infant?"

Fran immediately said, "Yes." This started the journey towards the adoption of their daughter, Nicoleta.

The process of adopting Nicoleta was far from easy. In fact, it was probably the hardest adoption that Fran and Sonny ever had. There were many aggravating phone calls as they were made to jump through hoops trying to get everything in order and there was always that looming thought that the adoption would fall through. The biggest problem they faced was getting their soon to be daughter her papers to travel. In Romania they didn't seem to understand that you couldn't offer someone a pack of cigarettes or money and have your papers stamped. So, at one point during this process the adoption attorney in Romania actually threatened to stay the adoption. After all money was sent, all paperwork was accounted for, and all provisions made, Fran now had to listen as her adoption facilitator relayed that the attorney was looking to keep her from her daughter. This didn't sit well with Fran and she asked her adoption facilitator to relay a message from her. "You tell him if he returns that baby, he will never get another child into this country because I will do everything in my power to accuse him and prove he sold a baby twice. Christian is not spelled S-T-U-P-I-D." This was the last time she was threatened and the adoption proceeded without further hindrance.

Throughout this process, although sometimes not easy, God had provided everything needed. Even when it came to picking up the newest addition to their family. During this exact same time, another couple also adopting a child from Romania, offered to bring Nicoleta home with them. In return for their kindness, Sonny and Fran offered to pay for one of their tickets. This also allowed Pastor Sonny to fulfill a commitment he had made to the church in Haiti.

When she saw Nicoleta arriving through the terminal, there was no doubting that this was the child who God spoke to her about in the car on that backroad. Wrapped in swaddling clothes and a babushka, with a bright red face and red scaly skin, Fran fell in love. It just so happened, the day Fran was called to pick up her child from the airport was the same day her friends were throwing her a baby shower. Overjoyed with her new daughter in her arms she headed back home to introduce Nicoleta to her new family.

"It was such an exciting time. The joy that filled the room was impossible to describe. My other kids were enthralled with her. The ladies from the church were overjoyed and my poor husband missed the whole thing. Yet when he returned from Haiti all it took was one look in the crib and from that day until now she has been his baby."

The Discovery

It was the summer of 1991. Fran and Sonny with their four adopted children including the newest member of the family, Nicoleta, headed to upstate New York to visit Fran's sister. As impossible as it is to believe, it was a different time. A time before seatbelts and car seats were mandatory. At one point during the trip Nicoleta was sitting on her mother's lap in the front seat. Without warning Nicoleta leaned forward and came back hitting Fran with such a shot in her right breast that it made her head spin. The impact was so forceful that it wasn't long before the area was covered by the purplish blue hues of the massive bruise which had formed. It was just a bruise and needed time to heal. But as time passed and the bruise didn't, Fran started to become concerned.

It was August of 1991, during a hurricane when Fran would make a discovery that would set in motion the prophecy which had been spoken years prior. Now given time to heal, Fran decided while in the shower to explore the bruise which had plagued her right breast for over a month. She discovered something that would shake her to her core. Feeling the big lump inside her breast made her sick to her stomach. There she stood in the shower with thoughts flooding her mind and fear beginning to take its hold. She immediately informed her husband. It would be some time before they would realize what a little lifesaver Nicoleta was.

The apparent progression of events had Fran go seek medical attention. She immediately had a mammogram, followed by a sonogram; for which the results of both were undetermined. After ruling out the possibility of a cyst, the doctors were still unsure, at this point, as to a diagnosis. All they were sure of, was that inside Fran's right breast lay a huge solid mass that needed the utmost attention.

Finding solace amidst the uncertainty of whether her worst fears were to be confirmed, was nearly impossible. Yet, even before she had found the lump and years before Nicoleta was adopted, God had already raised up someone through which He could demonstrate His love. Someone that would be there every step of Fran's Journey. She was one of Fran's oldest and most dear friends. Her name was Lorraine Sullivan and there is no doubt that she was handpicked by the Lord Himself for such a time. Once she heard that her friend's tests came back inconclusive Lorraine, being a nurse, immediately scheduled an appointment with the surgeon she worked with.

Lorraine accompanied Fran to the appointment and during the examination the doctor gave no indication as to his thoughts. However, by this time Fran had her suspicions. Lorraine discussed with the surgeon the best way to move forward. Fran had one condition and that was that she be back on her feet by September 8th. She had promised to give her son a birthday party and it wasn't a commitment she was prepared to break. So, with that in mind and the fact that the tumor was extremely massive, it was decided on the spot, that the best possible solution moving forward was to have a modified radical mastectomy. Before leaving, the surgeon asked to take a sample of the mass. Fran's positive response was followed by what looked like a ninety-foot needle being introduced into her right breast. The surgery was scheduled for September 3rd.

Be Anxious for Nothing

These had to be some of the worst days of her life. An unending cycle of being trapped inside her own mind with tormenting thoughts, abating any peace that once existed. She would muster every last ounce of energy she had, successfully not letting on to her children that she was completely wrecked inside. From the moment the last child was put on the bus for school in the morning, Fran tried her best to keep her thoughts from escaping her by continuously listening to worship music. Although this provided some comfort, it seemed it was Satan's intention to completely shipwreck Fran's faith. There were many questions that flooded her mind, and they came in quicker than she could process. However, there was one which stood out as a lingering thorn. Rightfully so and completely justified in her concern; she just couldn't put it out of her mind.

Fran and her husband Sonny, had four adopted children by this time. Manikam, Daniel, Caleb and Nicoleta. It wasn't a fear of dying that tangled with her spirit, but rather the thought that she would be leaving her husband behind to care for all these children by himself. That these children which God miraculously placed in their home would have to grow up without a mother. That she wouldn't be there to help her husband and be there for him when needed. The thought of never being able to see her older children grow up, get married and find happiness. Never getting to see

God's perfect will fulfilled in each of their lives. Never again getting to say those words "I love you". Never again. There were too many 'never agains'. There was such a battle for her mind that nothing short of the Lord granting miraculous peace would remedy it. So, in her most disheartened and restless moment the Lord came and rescued her.

Still over a week out from her surgery, laying there on the couch, Fran tried to focus on the words of the worship music she had playing in the background. Teetering, like on a seesaw, between trusting in God and unrelenting anxiety. It seemed as anxiety was the heavier of the two and just when she thought things couldn't get any worse, she received a phone call.

The phone call came from one of Fran's dearest friends who happened to be going through a detrimental family crisis. This conversation completely bankrupted any hope that Fran was clinging to. It was the proverbial straw that broke the camel's back. In the moments after hanging up the phone, Fran laid on the couch and with all hope lost, she called out, "Jesus!"

It was like a wave of the Lord's all-encompassing love had instantly washed over her. A message from the Lord where the perceptible reassurance of His embrace couldn't be any more real. In the instant that Fran called out to Jesus, He met her in a supernatural moment which lasted through the rest of her journey. Instant peace overcame all anxiety.

Now with a very tangible feeling of the Lord's presence, Fran was in a perfect place. The questions that plagued her thoughts prior were dismissed in place of a steady stream of reassuring statements that her God had everything under control.

He knew this would happen. Nothing takes the Lord by surprise.

These are just some of the statements that Fran now held fast to. One of the biggest revelations was the extent to which God intervened. Nicoleta to this day is an ever constant reminder of the sovereignty of the Lord Jesus Christ and how what we perceive insignificant moments, are just another avenue to which God is willing to show how much He cares.

If it's Cancer

The morning of the surgery, the surgeon spent some time talking with Fran, her husband and her best friend Lorraine. He explained to them the procedure and made them aware of the very real possibility that Fran may come out of anesthesia to find her body radically altered. The doctor said, "If I'm out in an hour, it means everything is fine; but over that, it is cancer and we will have to remove your breast."

Fran now being at perfect peace, said, "I understand and I am ok with it."

Fran found herself laying on the operating table with the surgeon holding her hand. All of a sudden she felt this warm feeling overcoming her body.

She said, "Whoa, what did you put in there?"

He responded, "Where do you like to go on vacation?"

"Palm Coast."

"Well go there."

Waking up in the recovery room, Fran heard the distant sounds of a child crying and chatter from people in the hospital. Coming out of the anesthesia, it was nice to see the familiar faces of her husband and her best friend waiting, later to be joined by her sister.

The next day the doctor came in and told Fran she wasn't to be raising her arm. Unbeknownst to him, she had already brushed her hair and took a walk, with an older lady, while dragging her I.V. next to her. Slowly taking off the dressing, the doctor and nurse kept an eye on Fran's face looking for any sign of emotional distress, but couldn't find any. Once the bandage was completely removed and the sight of the staples running from her chest to under her arm was fully exposed, the doctor once again looked for any reaction. Fran still at perfect peace wondered, *what do they want me to say?* So, she responded, "Nice job."

Shortly after the doctor left her room, Lorraine entered and mentioned that the doctor thought she was in denial and that she would break soon. *However, 'it's twenty-five years since then and he's still waiting'.* The next day she went home, returning a day later to have her chest tube removed. While back at the hospital, her friend mentioned that the hospital received a letter from a woman who was extremely angry. Her complaint was that she didn't receive any professional assistance while in the hospital, but instead needed to ask a woman who had a mastectomy, dragging around her I.V., to help her. Before leaving the doctor said, "Don't go playing any soccer." By this time they must have thought Fran was completely off her rocker, but what they didn't understand was the loving peace of Fran's Lord and Savior, Jesus Christ.

"The Lord was just so merciful, kind, perfect and generous. He was everything I could possibly need, want and more. I was feeling wonderful, my spirit was great. Forty-seven years of pain, hurt, sadness and every other negative emotion was gone and the love of God I felt during that whole period was just amazing. The only way I could describe it was; it was just me and Jesus in a bubble. Absolutely wonderful."

God's grace continued to encompass Fran through her chemotherapy over the next six months. Every step of the way her husband and her best friend were there to be a perfect demonstration of the Lord's love for her. From the smallest needs to spending hours bedside praying for her recovery, every physical and emotional need was met. By the very last treatment she started to feel a bit sick and weary. To which the doctor said, "It's like running a marathon and you're at the finish line." With that, the Lord had been true to His promise to her. That promise made years prior amidst a congregation in her home.

"What if I had disobeyed when the Lord told me to adopt?"

"What if we didn't go to Romania? What if we didn't get Nicoleta?"

"Would I have found the lump on my own? Would I still be here?"

"I can honestly say I don't believe I would be. She is indeed a miracle child. I can only say if the Lord is prompting you to do something, do it, it could be the difference between life and death."

Frances Confusione

THE WIDOW'S OLIVE OIL

The wife of a man from the company of the prophets cried out to Elisha, "Your servant my husband is dead, and you know that he revered the LORD. But now his creditor is coming to take my two boys as his slaves."

Elisha replied to her, "How can I help you? Tell me, what do you have in your house?"

"Your servant has nothing there at all," she said, "except a small jar of olive oil."

Elisha said, "Go around and ask all your neighbors for empty jars. Don't ask for just a few. Then go inside and shut the door behind you and your sons. Pour oil into all the jars, and as each is filled, put it to one side."

She left him and shut the door behind her and her sons. They brought the jars to her and she kept pouring. When all the jars were full, she said to her son, "Bring me another one."

But he replied, "There is not a jar left." Then the oil stopped flowing.

She went and told the man of God, and he said, "Go, sell the oil and pay your debts. You and your sons can live on what is left."

2 Kings 4:1-7 (NIV)

ꝏ 83 ON 83 ꝏ

Daniel awaited eagerly for his brother's phone call. It wasn't often that they had the chance to talk, but when they did it was always nice. What was particularly special about this call was that David was going to be sharing some of his testimonies for the book Daniel was writing. This one you're reading right now.

The phone rang and following small talk David got right into telling countless stories involving moments when God intervened in his life. Daniel listened as story after story was told. David is never shy to acknowledge how much God has been there in his time of need nor reluctant in attributing much to his parents' prayers for him over the years.

Daniel listened on the other end of the phone as one story seemed to be more exciting than the next. First, he spoke of one winter while driving, when he began sliding on black ice at more than 60 miles per hour and how God brought his car safely to a full stop, just before what in all likelihood would have been a fatal crash. Then another where he and a friend miraculously walked away without as much as a single scratch from an accident which should have ended in certain death. He next spoke of God's provision when he was forced to jump from the second story of a building which caught fire. Lastly, David spoke of an astonishing story, a true testament to how much our Savior loves us, in which God looked into the future and made provision for David years before it would be needed. Certainly, no coincidence.

Like many in their early twenties, David would typically spend his weekends hanging out with friends. However, one weekend would have ended differently were it not for the loving intervention of his Heavenly Father.

It was just past 2:00am when David and his two friends left the club. They jumped into his brand new Mercury Cougar and hopped on route 83 heading towards home. Route 83 can be a long monotonous road during the day. That monotony is that much more compounded with hardly anyone on the road past midnight. The street lights flickered as David passed them going more than 80 miles per hour. Then he hit the endless stretch where no lights lined the road. Where the only lights seen were the headlights of oncoming traffic. With his friends asleep in the backseat, there wasn't even the pleasure of conversation to break the insipidness of this ride. And with that, David's eyes closed.

Startled, David jolted awake to find himself heading through a curved section of the road where the guardrail was missing, careening towards a ditch at over 80 mph. Happening so fast, there was little time to think. Pure adrenaline took over. David quickly swerved to avoid fatally wrecking in a ditch and ended up darting back out on the road from another twenty-foot missing section of the guardrail. Had one of those two sections not been missing, David could safely say he probably wouldn't be alive to tell this story.

"At that speed, one of two things would have happened. The first, we would have come to an immediate stop on the guardrail, from over 80 mph to 0 in less than a second, or would have flipped over the guardrail and bent the car around a tree before landing in a ditch, both which would have been most likely fatal."

He said a quick little thanks to God for protecting him, but wouldn't know the true extent to which God intervened until a few days later.

A few days later, David was traveling down the same road. It was impossible to drive on this road and not recall that he'd almost lost his life just a few nights ago. He quickly noticed that the guardrails stretched for nearly the entire length of the road that he drove home that night. However, the only two missing twenty-foot sections were those which saved his life. It was interesting to ponder such questions:

What were the chances that I would fall asleep at just the right time?

What were the chances it would be that particular spot in the road?

Or better yet, what were the chances that those two missing guardrails would be spaced apart just enough to allow my car, doing over 80mph, to enter in one and exit the other?

All reasonable questions, but in the end David had to admit that absolutely nothing was left to chance, but rather it was God. Whether those two sections were purposely left missing several years before when constructed or removed sometime after for another reason, God had His reason. God honored David's parents' prayers and made sure David had a way where plausibly shouldn't have been, and because of that, David now has an amazing story which serves as a testament to God's limitless love.

God is our refuge and strength, an ever-present help in trouble.

Psalm 46:1 (NIV)

DANIEL IN THE DEN OF LIONS

It pleased Darius to appoint 120 satraps to rule throughout the kingdom, with three administrators over them, one of whom was Daniel. The satraps were made accountable to them so that the king might not suffer loss. Now Daniel so distinguished himself among the administrators and the satraps by his exceptional qualities that the king planned to set him over the whole kingdom. At this, the administrators and the satraps tried to find grounds for charges against Daniel in his conduct of government affairs, but they were unable to do so. They could find no corruption in him, because he was trustworthy and neither corrupt nor negligent. Finally these men said, "We will never find any basis for charges against this man Daniel unless it has something to do with the law of his God."

So these administrators and satraps went as a group to the king and said: "May King Darius live forever! The royal administrators, prefects, satraps, advisers and governors have all agreed that the king should issue an edict and enforce the decree that anyone who prays to any god or human being during the next thirty days, except to you, Your Majesty, shall be thrown into the lions' den. Now, Your Majesty, issue the decree and put it in writing so that it cannot be altered—in accordance with the law of the Medes and Persians, which cannot be repealed." So King Darius put the decree in writing.

Now when Daniel learned that the decree had been published, he went home to his upstairs room where the windows opened toward Jerusalem. Three times a day he got down on his knees and prayed, giving thanks to his God, just as he had done before. Then these men went as a group and found Daniel praying and asking God for help. So they went to the king and spoke to him about his royal decree: "Did you not publish a decree that during the next thirty days anyone who prays to any god or human being except to you, Your Majesty, would be thrown into the lions' den?"

The king answered, "The decree stands—in accordance with the law of the Medes and Persians, which cannot be repealed."

Then they said to the king, "Daniel, who is one of the exiles from Judah, pays no attention to you, Your Majesty, or to the decree you put in writing. He still prays three times a day." When the king heard this, he was greatly distressed; he was determined to rescue Daniel and made every effort until sundown to save him.

Then the men went as a group to King Darius and said to him, "Remember, Your Majesty, that according to the law of the Medes and Persians no decree or edict that the king issues can be changed."

So the king gave the order, and they brought Daniel and threw him into the lions' den. The king said to Daniel, "May your God, whom you serve continually, rescue you!"

A stone was brought and placed over the mouth of the den, and the king sealed it with his own signet ring and with the rings of his nobles, so that Daniel's situation might not be changed. Then the king returned to his palace and spent the night without eating and without any entertainment being brought to him. And he could not sleep.

At the first light of dawn, the king got up and hurried to the lions' den. When he came near the den, he called to Daniel in an anguished voice, "Daniel, servant of the living God, has your God, whom you serve continually, been able to rescue you from the lions?"

Daniel answered, "May the king live forever! My God sent his angel, and he shut the mouths of the lions. They have not hurt me, because I was found innocent in his sight. Nor have I ever done any wrong before you, Your Majesty."

The king was overjoyed and gave orders to lift Daniel out of the den. And when Daniel was lifted from the den, no wound was found on him, because he had trusted in his God.

At the king's command, the men who had falsely accused Daniel were brought in and thrown into the lions' den, along with their wives and children. And before they reached the floor of the den, the lions overpowered them and crushed all their bones.

Then King Darius wrote to all the nations and peoples of every language in all the earth:

"May you prosper greatly!

"I issue a decree that in every part of my kingdom people must fear and reverence the God of Daniel.

"For He is the living God and He endures forever; His kingdom will not be destroyed, His dominion will never end. He rescues and he saves; He performs signs and wonders in the heavens and on the earth. He has rescued Daniel from the power of the lions."

So Daniel prospered during the reign of Darius and the reign of Cyrus the Persian.

Daniel Chapter 6 (NIV)

Ꙍ MARIE'S SON Ꙍ

At forty-two, having already had four children of which the youngest was thirteen, Marie was surprised to discover she was expecting another. There was no denying the results of that clear blue pregnancy test which rested briefly on her bathroom counter. In less than nine months Marie would be welcoming her fifth child to this world.

All through her pregnancy the OBGYN continually pestered her to have testing done, due to her age. However, she kindly paid her no mind. She figured "if God was going to bless me with my fifth child at forty-two, I was going to welcome this child no matter what." On the day Marie gave birth to her son, things seemed to progress slowly. But finally, at 1:45 p.m. on September 21, 1999, Liam B. Rooney greeted the world. Marie greatly anticipated that moment when her new baby would be placed in her arms. However, before she could even greet her new child he was quickly whisked away, for testing, by the neonatal team.

After forty-minutes of wondering what was happening and how her child was doing, Marie finally spoke up. She asked them what was wrong. She surely thought whatever it was, was going to be horrible. With her heart in her stomach, she waited for one of the nurses to get the doctor. The doctor walked through the door. The anxiety Marie felt at this moment was indescribable. Many thoughts had entered her mind while she waited for the doctor and now he was here. The doctor walked to her bedside. The look on his face told Marie something wasn't right. In a professional yet sympathetic tone, he said, "We believe your son has Down syndrome."

Relief came over Marie. She responded, "That's all? Would you please bring me my baby so I can hold and kiss him?" The whole staff was also relieved and surprised by Marie's response to this news. News of other complications followed such as low oxygen saturation levels, jaundice, and a questionable heart irregularity, which the team monitored closely. Finally, after hours of waiting, Marie at last was able to hold her child in her arms and welcome Liam into the world.

One week later, Liam was evaluated by a pediatric cardiologist in Stonybrook Hospital on Long Island. This visit would be one that, even to this day, Marie could remember as if it happened yesterday. The cardiologist, much to Marie's surprise, told her that Liam had a very severe heart defect and that nothing could be done for him. He said, "Take him home and make him comfortable."

Marie walked out of the hospital utterly numb. After placing Liam in the car, she took her seat behind the steering wheel and completely unraveled. For over ten minutes Marie uncontrollably screamed and cried.

"I was so heartbroken. How could this be true? God blessed me with this beautiful baby and now he was going to take him back!"

Once home, after speaking with some nurses she worked with, Marie was given the phone number to another pediatric cardiologist, Dr. R.S. This doctor was without a doubt picked by God's loving hand because this doctor offered something back that Marie had had taken from her, and that was hope. During the meeting with this cardiologist, Marie was finally given the answer she needed to hear. That being that Liam was going to survive.

After countless sleepless nights, congestive heart failure twice and numerous other setbacks, Liam's surgery was finally scheduled for February 14, 2000. Marie humbly prayed that God would guide the hands of the surgeon and that prayer didn't return void. Such a complicated and intricate surgery involving not only Liam's heart but also his liver and lungs was estimated to take a minimum of eight hours. During the surgery, the surgeon had to construct heart valves and flaps. In addition, the surgeon carefully patched two quarter sized holes in the heart of this baby who was no more than five months old. Oh, and it only took three hours.

"What a miracle this was. God not only blessed me with my fifth child, but He also guided me in the direction I needed to go. I am forever thankful to God. When I thought all was lost, God showed me that He never ignores our prayers. He answered every prayer I prayed. Not only that, the fact that He chose me to have Liam makes me feel special in His eyes."

"Liam is now seventeen and doing well. He shows me every day just how great God's promises are."

Marie Rooney

JESUS HEALS AN OFFICIAL'S SON

After the two days he left for Galilee. (Now Jesus himself had pointed out that a prophet has no honor in his own country.) When he arrived in Galilee, the Galileans welcomed him. They had seen all that he had done in Jerusalem at the Passover Festival, for they also had been there.

Once more he visited Cana in Galilee, where he had turned the water into wine. And there was a certain royal official whose son lay sick at Capernaum. When this man heard that Jesus had arrived in Galilee from Judea, he went to him and begged him to come and heal his son, who was close to death.

"Unless you people see signs and wonders," Jesus told him, "you will never believe."

The royal official said, "Sir, come down before my child dies."

"Go," Jesus replied, "your son will live."

The man took Jesus at his word and departed. While he was still on the way, his servants met him with the news that his boy was living. When he inquired as to the time when his son got better, they said to him, "Yesterday, at one in the afternoon, the fever left him."

Then the father realized that this was the exact time at which Jesus had said to him, "Your son will live." So he and his whole household believed.

This was the second sign Jesus performed after coming from Judea to Galilee.

John 4:43-54 (NIV)

ⓠ WINDOW PAIN ⓠ

All of us at one time or another have had that feeling: you're compelled to act, even if it appears to defy all reason. It's that moment when a driver is compelled to switch lanes only to narrowly miss being involved in an accident. It's the time when, for no reason at all, you decide to call your friend only to discover she's in need of prayer. It's that moment when God Himself seems to tap you lovingly on the shoulder and gently whisper to your spirit that action needs to be taken. Some will chalk it up to coincidence or a 6th sense. Others may stake it on being lucky or at the right place at the right time. However, for any true believer in Christ, it's nothing short of the Lord speaking to us on our behalf or on behalf of someone else. Fran knows this only too well as one particular summer afternoon would have spelt horror had it not been for that feeling.

It was a beautiful sunny morning. With worship music playing in the background, Fran was in great spirits. She now had been cancer free for some time and still couldn't believe how tangible the Lord's presence was throughout her whole ordeal. With the older children at school and Nicoleta down for a nap, Fran now had some freedom to get some chores accomplished around the house.

After sweeping the kitchen, she began to clean the dishes out of the sink in preparation of washing the floor. However, no sooner did she pick up the first dish, did she feel an extreme sinking feeling in the pit of her stomach. At first she brushed it off, nothing of concern. But when that feeling continued, she paid it more attention. That's when she felt the Lord tell her to quickly check on Nicoleta.

The clanging sound from the dish being dropped in the sink could have been heard throughout the house. Fran raced up the stairs and into the bedroom to check on Nicoleta. But when she looked in the crib, Nicoleta couldn't be found. She immediately checked the adjacent room and there looking back at Fran was Nicoleta with a big smile on her face. Fran stood there in horror as she watched her baby girl precariously sitting on the windowsill, rocking back and forth through the open second story window of their Long Island home. One of her other children must have left the window open and without a screen, there was nothing to prevent Nicoleta from plummeting backwards twenty feet to her death.

Fran couldn't pray to the Lord fast enough in her mind, "Lord, let her not fall, let her not fall, let her not fall!" But she tried her best to not let on the complete horror she was in, as she inched towards her. Seven feet, six feet, and then five. Every foot seemed like a million miles. A moment so surreal it could have been a dream. As Fran continued to approach her daughter, talking in a normal tone, she engaged Nicoleta in conversation to keep her from swinging. Then finally when Fran was just within three feet, Nicoleta swung her legs up and began to fall backwards. But just then her mother grabbed her and pulled her quickly in the window and closed it.

Fran sat next to the window, on the floor, with Nicoleta in her arms for some time. It took quite a few minutes to decompress from all that had just happened. During that whole time she could not stop thanking God for giving her such a clear and urgent impression that Nicoleta was in danger. From that moment, not one day has gone by where Fran isn't constantly reminded of God's continued sovereign intervention in her life.

EUTYCHUS RAISED FROM THE DEAD AT TROAS

On the first day of the week we came together to break bread. Paul spoke to the people and, because he intended to leave the next day, kept on talking until midnight. There were many lamps in the upstairs room where we were meeting. Seated in a window was a young man named Eutychus, who was sinking into a deep sleep as Paul talked on and on. When he was sound asleep, he fell to the ground from the third story and was picked up dead. Paul went down, threw himself on the young man and put his arms around him. "Don't be alarmed," he said. "He's alive!" Then he went upstairs again and broke bread and ate. After talking until daylight, he left. The people took the young man home alive and were greatly comforted.

Acts 20:7-12 (NIV)

⓪ RED LIGHT, GREEN LIGHT ⓪

Insanity, complete insanity!" Ryan said to himself as he tried to maneuver his vehicle around another on a road barely meant to accommodate two lanes of traffic. What was even more senseless was that a driver's life was fully dependent on a series of flashes. A crazy line of communication between a driver and oncoming vehicles, but it seemed to work.

Ryan had been in Mexico for some time now and had familiarized himself with various aspects of (Organization's name withheld). However, there was still one experience that had eluded him. But not this day. This day would forever be marked in his memory as the beginning of one of the biggest learning experiences of his lifetime. An experience marked by fear and apprehension; shortly followed by trust, courage, hope, faith and fulfillment. An adventure of sorts.

Finding himself in the shoes of those he used to read about. Those people risking everything on the front lines in an effort to help those in need. Ryan had never imagined the events that would play out when he was asked by Chris to accompany him on a trip to Brownsville, Texas.

It was well before the sun could be seen peeking over the horizon. Ryan and Chris loaded the van with some of their belongings and set out on their mission towards Brownsville. This was going to be an experience which would force growth on many different levels. The purpose for their trip was to retrieve medical supplies for the mobile medical ministry operated in Mexico City. Chris had made this trip too many times to count, but for Ryan this was his first. Ryan had no apprehensions about the trip, in spite of Chris explaining the possible risks. He also, was no stranger to being in dangerous situations; however, this would be an experience unlike any other.

It was a big vehicle. Room enough to accommodate Ryan, Chris and all the medical supplies they needed to bring back with them. It was of an older model, but had a few features not typical of your normal vehicle. That's because this van was designed to smuggle items across the border. The ceiling subtly sat lower than one would assume judging by the exterior of the vehicle and that was because what Ryan and Chris were about to do could very well land them, for a long time, in a Mexican prison for drug smuggling. A small compartment was designed between the roof of the van and the inside ceiling. This is where the medical supplies were going to be hidden. When transporting medicine and other supplies across the border, typically they are accompanied by a doctor or letter listing all inventory and showing valid authorization for transport. Ryan and Chris had neither, but were exceedingly resolute in making it to Brownsville despite any dangers that may await them on their return.

The journey to Brownsville took two days and had its fair share of excitement. As if the ever present thought of being caught with medical contraband on the way back wasn't enough, Ryan and Chris were continually aware of the Federales. They were the Federal Mexican police. In fact, it wasn't bandits or criminals that posed the greatest threat, but rather corrupt Mexican police officers. Without warning they would be behind you, lights flashing, signaling for you to pull over. Most times a person was given two choices. Bribe or jail. Ryan was only too familiar with this, having had a recent experience himself. But of all the dangers on their journey, the most constantly imposing was that of trying to maneuver their vehicle amidst the traffic flow.

The drive through northern Mexico featured the rugged landscape of the country's arid desert environment. A much different experience than Ryan's many trips through Mexico's southern subtropics. It was over 600 miles of road barely wide enough to accommodate both directions of traffic. A highway, if you could call it that, riddled with inherent dangers. The perfect convergence of circumstances vigorously set on trying to take one's life and here on this road Ryan was forced to drive like he never drove before.

Keeping up with the flow of traffic was far from the appropriate phrase that one would use to describe driving conditions. In fact, there wasn't a flow at all. Mexico's regulations are extremely lax, especially when compared to those of their neighbor to the north. So, without inspection requirements or safety regulations, there are many vehicles, if that's what you could still call them, creating dangerous conditions for other drivers. The main problem being that many of these vehicles cannot reach speeds of more than 10-20 mph. So when approaching, a driver has no choice but to pass and this is no simple task.

The language was universally known. At least, that was the assumption. A little bit of faith never hurt either but it was still a very precarious line of communication. When a driver wished to pass another vehicle, he would slowly maneuver his car out from behind the one he wished to pass and flash his lights consecutively to signal the vehicle to move over. Since the road was too narrow, the most any vehicle being passed could move would result with half the vehicle still in the road. Once that vehicle moved over as far as possible, the driver wishing to pass would frantically flash his lights to signal to oncoming traffic that they had to move over as far as possible also. This created just enough room to allow a driver to pass another. Close calls were common place on these roads. Something Ryan also had experienced on this trip.

With Chris fast asleep, laying across the back seat, Ryan was now behind the wheel. He quickly learned that absent of conversation, this trip was very long and monotonous. It took everything in Ryan to keep from zoning out driving through the repetitive desert landscape, but he was happy to do it, as Chris was overdue for a rest.

It was no longer than forty-five minutes into his drive when Ryan noticed he was quickly approaching an old rusty truck. The truck was traveling at no more than fifteen-mph and with Ryan approaching at over fifty it was pretty clear that Ryan was going to have to pass. As he approached the vehicle he began to flash his lights and honk the horn. The truck quickly moved over as far as he could. As Ryan slowly accelerated around the truck he frantically started flashing his lights to the approaching truck to do the same. However, what was approaching was a tractor trailer. Ryan knew it was going to be a tight squeeze, but now it was too late to turn back. With the tractor trailer moved as far over as possible, Ryan maneuvered his van through the vehicles.

His heart would have been in his stomach had there been time to register the situation, but everything happened too fast. Following the loud crashing sound of the driver's side mirror being forcefully torn from its mount, Ryan saw Chris' head pop up in the rearview mirror. The look on his face to this day, is one that Ryan can recall as if it happened just yesterday. The exposed metal scratch that ran along the side of their van, was more than enough proof to validate the belated terror that befell them. Now, looking at the terrified look on Chris' face staring back in horror through the rearview mirror, Ryan said with a slight chuckle, "It was a little tight." Chris exhaled with a sigh of relief as he turned to look back at the mirror bouncing erratically on the road behind them. All being told, with the exception of this near collision, the ride to Brownsville was pretty uneventful. They even seemed to have favor with all the checkpoints.

When pulling up to a checkpoint, there was a signal light meant to direct drivers. If it flashed red, this signaled drivers to pull over and be prepared to spend an hour or more being searched. Ryan and Chris managed to hit all green lights on the way up, allowing them to pass undeterred. Now with the last checkpoint behind them and only minutes from the Texas border, it wouldn't be long before they reached their destination. A little church in Brownsville.

It was hard to believe that this little place would be the center of such a big enterprise. This church acted as a central hub for medical supply donations coming from the United States, Canada, as well as the rest of the world, into Mexico. The church sat geographically perfect, being close enough to the Texas-Mexico border, to minimize travel time while being far enough to abate any suspicions of their activities.

Ryan and Chris arrived early afternoon of their second day of travel. As they approached the church, they were extremely grateful to be greeted by many, who seemed only too pleased to have them joining them for the night. Although all talk seemed casual as plans were being discussed about how the medical supplies were being transported, everyone knew this was no light matter. Tomorrow, Ryan and Chris would set out and attempt to cross the border with medical contraband and if caught, they could only pray a bribe would suffice to avoid being imprisoned.

The sun barely had a chance to warm the earth when Ryan and Chris walked outside to find their vehicle was already being loaded. It was more than just making good time as to the reason for an early start. Typically, the checkpoint guards were more likely to let vehicles pass through earlier in the morning, and this was something they intended to use to their advantage. So with a quick farewell, Ryan and Chris set out on their trip back to Mexico.

Ryan and Chris were in incredible spirits this morning. They couldn't help but feel that God was on their side. Being spared the almost certain trouble with the Federales and passing through all checkpoints on the way up, reaffirmed the idea that God was going to make this trip a breeze. Crossing over into Mexico, Ryan and Chris said a quick prayer, which was more of an act of faith, thanking God in advance for letting them through all checkpoints they would have to pass. And with that, the first checkpoint was in sight.

As they approached the checkpoint, Ryan noticed that the light flashed green for every car ahead of them. Ryan and Chris smiled at each other. Normally, they would have been nervous, but they were so sure God was going to make this trip easy. With the car ahead of them given a green light, Ryan inched up their van and prepared to continue driving. But to their utter dismay, the light turned red. Their hearts shot past their stomachs and rolled on the floor. As they pulled off to the side of the road all they could do was pray. What made it worse was during the day the seam that allowed access to the hidden compartment in the ceiling was visible for anyone looking.

Within seconds of pulling off, Ryan and Chris were ripped from their vehicle and searched. Every pocket of their clothing was emptied and every piece of documentation was verified. After searching Ryan and Chris, they turned their attention to the vehicle. The nervous beads of sweat that formed on Ryan's forehead would have ran down his face had the dry desert wind not wisped them away. One of the checkpoint officers opened the back of a truck revealing two drug sniffing dogs, who seemed only too eager to do their job. Checkpoint security meticulously inspected every inch and crevice of their vehicle. With the use of mirrors and various other tools anyone could tell they knew for what and where to look. When Ryan noticed them checking inside the tires and unscrewing the gas cap, he thought for sure he would be making his next call to his parents from a Mexican prison, asking them to contact an international attorney.

They both nervously looked on as the inside of their van was searched. Every vent and door panel pulled. All the seating thoroughly inspected. Even the flooring pulled up to check for hidden contraband. After roughly an hour and forty-five minutes, Ryan and Chris glanced at each other as if to say without saying, "we may actually make it through this." With that, one of the officers signaled to the officer watching Ryan and Chris that they could return to their vehicle. As the last officer headed to exit their vehicle, he hit his head on the ceiling. Ryan once again looked at Chris, as they froze for a moment; had the officer looked up he would have noticed something not right, but instead he rubbed his head and stepped out of their van. Ryan and Chris could hardly believe it. It was all they could talk about for the next hour.

Following this experience, with his adrenalin wearing off, it was as if all anxiety about being caught fled from Ryan also. The next checkpoints served no concern as he approached them. But fortunately they were given green lights and allowed to pass, safely returning with all the medical supplies needed.

Chimalhuacan

"I cannot begin to describe the landscape I see standing upon the shoulders of those who support me. I owe them far more than my weight." – Author Unknown

It wasn't uncommon for the ministry Ryan was involved in, Side Walk Sunday School, and the mobile medical clinic to work side by side. This was the case when visiting one of the poorest areas in Mexico City. An area in Chimalhuacan, otherwise known as Garbage City to the natives, because it was a landfill which many people called home.

"After the trip that Chris and I made to get the medical supplies, I'll never forget standing there watching the mobile medical clinic treat people. This was one of the very few times in my life where I feel I truly made a positive impact. Where my efforts and bravery made a difference."

"Green lights are always nice, but God receives more glory when the lights are red"

Ryan Confusione

ELISHA TRAPS BLINDED ARAMEANS

Now the king of Aram was at war with Israel. After conferring with his officers, he said, "I will set up my camp in such and such a place."

The man of God sent word to the king of Israel: "Beware of passing that place, because the Arameans are going down there." So the king of Israel checked on the place indicated by the man of God. Time and again Elisha warned the king, so that he was on his guard in such places.

This enraged the king of Aram. He summoned his officers and demanded of them, "Tell me! Which of us is on the side of the king of Israel?"

"None of us, my lord the king," said one of his officers, "but Elisha, the prophet who is in Israel, tells the king of Israel the very words you speak in your bedroom."

"Go, find out where he is," the king ordered, "so I can send men and capture him." The report came back: "He is in Dothan." Then he sent horses and chariots and a strong force there. They went by night and surrounded the city.

When the servant of the man of God got up and went out early the next morning, an army with horses and chariots had surrounded the city. "Oh no, my lord! What shall we do?" the servant asked.

"Don't be afraid," the prophet answered. "Those who are with us are more than those who are with them."

And Elisha prayed, "Open his eyes, LORD, so that he may see." Then the LORD opened the servant's eyes, and he looked and saw the hills full of horses and chariots of fire all around Elisha.

As the enemy came down toward him, Elisha prayed to the LORD, "Strike this army with blindness." So he struck them with blindness, as Elisha had asked.

Elisha told them, "This is not the road and this is not the city. Follow me, and I will lead you to the man you are looking for." And he led them to Samaria.

After they entered the city, Elisha said, "LORD, open the eyes of these men so they can see." Then the LORD opened their eyes and they looked, and there they were, inside Samaria.

When the king of Israel saw them, he asked Elisha, "Shall I kill them, my father? Shall I kill them?"

"Do not kill them," he answered. "Would you kill those you have captured with your own sword or bow? Set food and water before them so that they may eat and drink and then go back to their master." So he prepared a great feast for them, and after they had finished eating and drinking, he sent them away, and they returned to their master. So the bands from Aram stopped raiding Israel's territory. 2 Kings 6:8-23 (NIV)

ɷ PASTOR WILSON'S VISION ɷ

It was just past midnight when Gladys was awakened by her husband's restlessness. She turned to find him profusely sweating. Distressing cries uttered from his mouth echoed throughout the house. Undoubtedly he was having a terrible dream, which for her husband, Pastor Roger 'Wilson' Charles, was a rare occurrence. In the past, anytime dreams presented intensity enough to cause her husband such distress, they were usually something that warranted attention.

Leaning in towards her husband, in an effort to awaken him, she gently pushed his shoulder and called his name. No such luck at first, but after a few attempts his eyes opened revealing utter distress. There was little chance of him getting back to sleep that night. After describing his dream to his wife, he spent the rest of the night knelt next to his bed, praying to God over this dream. Undoubtedly, it was a warning, a warning from God, but what was it?

He described: It was complete chaos and devastation. It began with a fire and this fire destroyed everything that it touched. An almost supernatural blaze. Taking on a life of its own, nothing could quench it. It wasn't long before he noticed the fire getting bigger, like a blanket racing across the country destroying everything in its wake. The fire consumed buildings, trees, and people. Even mountains were crumbling! He caught sight of many bulldozers pushing rubble and with it, the corpses of countless bodies. A river of blood ran throughout the city leaving evidence of its red pigment on everything it washed over. There was no discrimination among this force of destruction. Havoc was its name and with it travelled death and despair.

Standing in front of his church, he looked around to notice that this wave of destruction was quickly racing towards him. Buildings falling in procession, much like dominos, creeping ever closer as he helplessly watched. The sound of screaming, the crackling of fire and the dimmed sight of what remained of the surrounding buildings' silhouettes through the black veil of smoke which now enveloped the city was more than enough to overwhelm. He could feel the heat from the blaze on the surface of his arms and face, long after he awoke.

The overwhelming blaze burned extremely hot and grew larger as it raced across the country consuming everything. Watching one building after another being consumed, it was only a matter of time before this mammoth presence of fire stood in front of the church. Utter destruction now had surrounded the church. One would have thought this fire had an active consciousness saving the church building for last. This massive wave had grown almost too large to comprehend and with it now only feet from the church, Pastor Wilson could only expect the worst. Just as it seemed the church building would be but another destroyed victim to add to this fire's fury, it stopped. It was about this time he woke up, drenched in sweat, to the sound of his wife's voice calling his name. He awakened from a dream where his entire country was destroyed, all buildings as far as he could see laid in ruins except one. The church!

The next morning, having determined this was a clear warning from God, he set out with the purpose of sharing his dream with anyone who would listen. He began with his congregation. After sharing his dream, the whole church entered into three days of fasting and intercession. Following these three days, he arranged a meeting with the mayor. As Wilson shared his dream, she broke down in tears; understanding that if what this pastor had seen comes true, it would mean complete devastation to countless lives. She soon after called for a meeting. An assembly where over sixty pastors from all over the country would gather to hear what Pastor Wilson had to say. He was well received by all the pastors except one, who seemed to go out of his way to mock the vision's recipient. Pastor Wilson, himself, wasn't sure what his dream meant nor would he ever realize the full extent of how his obedience to walk out in faith would save lives. Over the next few weeks this dream continued to play over in his mind.

January 12, 2010 started out like any other day. Yet there was an eerie presence in the air. Something noticeably different but subtle enough to keep a person guessing. There are quite a few ministries that Pastor Wilson oversees and today he found himself in the city of Lartigue, in Haiti's mountains; where he established a children's ministry and school. He still couldn't go more than half a day without giving thoughts to the dream he'd had just a few weeks prior. Over the last few weeks he shared his dream with as many people as he came in contact with, and with gratitude most welcomed what he had to say. Wilson couldn't help but feel an urgency, and as the day progressed that feeling had grown stronger until there was no denying something was imminent.

On the eve of January 12, 2010 at 4:53 p.m., just southeast of the Haitian capital of Port-au-Prince, a massive earthquake, magnitude 7.0, struck the country of Haiti. Once it hit, there was no denying what God was trying to show him weeks earlier in his dream. The initial shock was absolutely devastating, but to add insult to injury, the aftershocks inflicted considerable damage as well. It was complete destruction, just as Pastor had seen in his dream. It seemed there was no safe place. Horror had come to this country and wasn't going to leave without taking its price.

Tuesday morning of January 12th was an exciting day for Pastor Wilson. It was the day he started to make the journey back from Lartigue to his hometown, Pétion-ville, Haiti. He couldn't wait to return home to see his wife and family. The trip was exceedingly long, but with an early enough start, he knew he could make it in a day's time. He looked forward to sleeping in his own bed that night. It wasn't long into his trip when Wilson heard the Lord tell him to stop at a hotel. It was a little puzzling seeing it was still early and there was plenty of daylight left to travel, but being obedient Pastor Wilson rented the room.

It was 4:53 p.m. while the Pastor was kneeling in prayer that he began to feel the floor shake under him. Shortly after, the door and drawers began to slide open and closed on their hinges as the shaking grew more intense. It was all Pastor Wilson could do to keep from falling into something. Once the initial shock had passed, he immediately tried to get in contact with his wife, to no avail. What brought even more concern, was when he heard that the National Palace had collapsed. He thought, surely if something as well built as the palace could collapse, his family would stand no chance in his house. So in desperation he continued to call until finally on Wednesday at 3:00 in the morning, he was able to hear his wife's voice on the other end of the line.

The call was bittersweet as Pastor Wilson listened to his wife's so familiar voice. Barely maintaining composure, Gladys described how, while on her way to the church for a prayer meeting the earth began to shake. She was only feet away, in a cab, as a supermarket was reduced to rubble with people inside. Pastor continued to listen as she spoke of the passing of their neighbors during the quake. It would be several days before Pastor Wilson would be able to reunite with his family.

Three days after the quake, Wilson found no choice but to leave his car stranded at the hotel and try to find another means of reaching his family. The earthquake had caused a river to flood cutting off the only safe route back home and without any relief efforts, Pastor Wilson wasn't sure if getting home was even possible.

Back in Florida, immediately after the earthquake, Pastor Sonny tried desperately to reach Wilson but establishing a connection was impossible. On the second day, a member of Pastor Wilson's church posted a message on social media, letting him know the family was safe. It would be one more day before Wilson would finally speak with Sonny and explain his situation. Feeling completely helpless, Sonny called everyone he could hoping to find some way of reuniting Wilson with his family. He was glad to hear, a few days later, that he was able to rent a motor taxi which could traverse another route home.

Once in his hometown of Pétion-ville, Wilson stopped his taxi in the middle of the rubble strewn streets and spent a few minutes looking around. He was immediately overwhelmed as he was forced to listen to the sounds of people yelling and crying. He caught sight of countless people searching through the rubble for friends and family members. Bodies lined the streets which still had a heavy cloud of dust from the tumbling buildings. Everyone was still extremely anxious with the uncertainty that another aftershock lay in wait to wreak more devastation. Wilson fell to his knees and couldn't help but cry. Nothing could have prepared him, not even that dream, for what had taken place just a few days ago in Haiti.

Once home, Wilson was extremely grateful to be reunited with his family, but the feeling was tempered with the knowledge that more than thirty-five members of his congregation had perished in the quakes, many whom were close personal friends. He also later received a call from another pastor, one who had heard him speak at the assembly put together by the mayor. In this call, the pastor explained that if it weren't for Wilson's sharing of his dream and taking time to fast and pray, many more people would have been lost. He continued by telling of the horrific death that the one pastor who openly mocked him during the meeting had suffered.

It was a very devastating time. Many lost family members and lifelong friends. Countless homes and businesses were reduced to nothing more than rubble and dust. Now government assured that the horror had passed, they began to assess the damage. One order of business was assessing all the buildings. Wilson wasn't too surprised to see the church building still standing, but what did amaze him was, just as in his dream, all the buildings surrounding the church had suffered irreparable damage. Following the quake, many buildings, especially those with concrete roofs were considered unsafe and condemned. This included the church building. The balcony of the church had to be removed due to structural damage and during this time the church couldn't be accessed. Always committed, Pastor Wilson met with his congregation under tents made of tarps and other materials that could be found. Many people came looking for food and water, as well as other needs to be met. So Pastor Wilson would spend hours every day for months, standing in lines among the United Nations and world food program relief efforts trying to get what little he could to bring back and when he wasn't standing in line, he was on the phone trying to find other means for help. Pastor admits, contrary to public opinion, it was churches and private donations in the United States, Canada and the rest of the world that were responsible for nearly all of the relief efforts in Haiti.

Today, standing in the church, Pastor Wilson is ever reminded of the countless years of loyalty from lifelong friends such as Pastor Sonny and those who stood faithfully with him. How through his ministry many have been housed, fed and clothed. A reminder that it was Sonny's faithfulness to God that would lead to the building of the church in Haiti and with many prayers all obstacles faded away. Just as in Wilson's dream, God had spared the building from certain destruction. This building now provides a sanctuary for many who, to this day, are still hungry, homeless and displaced due to the horrific events on January 12, 2010. Now when he looks out amidst his congregation he can't help but notice a long crack running down one of the walls, much like a scar, an ever constant reminder of God's faithfulness.

THE IMAGE OF GOLD AND THE BLAZING FURNACE

King Nebuchadnezzar made an image of gold, sixty cubits high and six cubits wide, and set it up on the plain of Dura in the province of Babylon. He then summoned the satraps, prefects, governors, advisers, treasurers, judges, magistrates and all the other provincial officials to come to the dedication of the image he had set up. So the satraps, prefects, governors, advisers, treasurers, judges, magistrates and all the other provincial officials assembled for the dedication of the image that King Nebuchadnezzar had set up, and they stood before it.

Then the herald loudly proclaimed, "Nations and peoples of every language, this is what you are commanded to do: As soon as you hear the sound of the horn, flute, zither, lyre, harp, pipe and all kinds of music, you must fall down and worship the image of gold that King Nebuchadnezzar has set up. Whoever does not fall down and worship will immediately be thrown into a blazing furnace."

Therefore, as soon as they heard the sound of the horn, flute, zither, lyre, harp and all kinds of music, all the nations and peoples of every language fell down and worshiped the image of gold that King Nebuchadnezzar had set up.

At this time some astrologers came forward and denounced the Jews. They said to King Nebuchadnezzar, "May the king live forever! Your Majesty has issued a decree that everyone who hears the sound of the horn, flute, zither, lyre, harp, pipe and all kinds of music must fall down and worship the image of gold, and that whoever does not fall down and worship will be thrown into a blazing furnace. But there are some Jews whom you have set over the affairs of the province of Babylon—Shadrach, Meshach and Abednego—who pay no attention to you, Your Majesty. They neither serve your gods nor worship the image of gold you have set up."

Furious with rage, Nebuchadnezzar summoned Shadrach, Meshach and Abednego. So these men were brought before the king, and Nebuchadnezzar said to them, "Is it true, Shadrach, Meshach and Abednego, that you do not serve my gods or worship the image of gold I have set up? Now when you hear the sound of the horn, flute, zither, lyre, harp, pipe and all kinds of music, if you are ready to fall down and worship the image I made, very good. But if you do not worship it, you will be thrown immediately into a blazing furnace. Then what god will be able to rescue you from my hand?"

Shadrach, Meshach and Abednego replied to him, "King Nebuchadnezzar, we do not need to defend ourselves before you in this matter. If we are thrown into the blazing furnace, the God we serve is able to deliver us from it, and he will deliver us from Your Majesty's hand. But even if he does not, we want you to know, Your Majesty that we will not serve your gods or worship the image of gold you have set up."

Then Nebuchadnezzar was furious with Shadrach, Meshach and Abednego, and his attitude toward them changed. He ordered the furnace heated seven times hotter than usual and commanded some of the strongest soldiers in his army to tie up Shadrach, Meshach and Abednego and throw them into the blazing furnace. So these men, wearing their robes, trousers, turbans and other clothes, were bound and thrown into the blazing furnace. The king's command was so urgent and the furnace so hot that the flames of the fire killed the soldiers who took up Shadrach, Meshach and Abednego, and these three men, firmly tied, fell into the blazing furnace.

Then King Nebuchadnezzar leaped to his feet in amazement and asked his advisers, "Weren't there three men that we tied up and threw into the fire?"

They replied, "Certainly, Your Majesty."

He said, "Look! I see four men walking around in the fire, unbound and unharmed, and the fourth looks like a son of the gods."

Nebuchadnezzar then approached the opening of the blazing furnace and shouted, "Shadrach, Meshach and Abednego, servants of the Most High God, come out! Come here!"

So Shadrach, Meshach and Abednego came out of the fire, and the satraps, prefects, governors and royal advisers crowded around them. They saw that the fire had not harmed their bodies, nor was a hair of their heads singed; their robes were not scorched, and there was no smell of fire on them.

Then Nebuchadnezzar said, "Praise be to the God of Shadrach, Meshach and Abednego, who has sent his angel and rescued his servants! They trusted in him and defied the king's command and were willing to give up their lives rather than serve or worship any god except their own God. Therefore I decree that the people of any nation or language who say anything against the God of Shadrach, Meshach and Abednego be cut into pieces and their houses be turned into piles of rubble, for no other god can save in this way."

Then the king promoted Shadrach, Meshach and Abednego in the province of Babylon.

Daniel Chapter 3 (NIV)

ᏇᎧ WHEN GOD SPEAKS ᏇᎧ

Having already adopted a child, Sonny and Fran's pastor thought they might be interested in an adoption agency he was familiar with in South Carolina. It seemed like a perfect fit considering this agency specialized in ethnically diverse adoptions and their only adopted son happened to be Indian. So, after some inquiring, Sonny and Fran were a little disheartened to hear that they were considered ineligible to adopt due to their age. They thought that perhaps God was opening a door for them to add yet another member to their family, but it seemed that door was closed. The events that shortly proceeded would later confirm their understanding that when God opens a door, nothing nor no one can shut it.

Setting aside the normal Christmas traditions of putting up a tree and spending time with family at home,

Sonny and Fran decided this year they would take their family on a Christmas vacation. It was going to be a joyous time of year like all the previous, however this one would be spent in PTL, South Carolina. So, with family in procession, Sonny and Fran led the tailgate from Long Island, New York to South Carolina.

The best way to describe PTL is that it was a resort of sorts, but much more. It was a very unique place to vacation because it offered something for everyone. Over the years it would become a nostalgic destination where great memories and friends were made. To this day many can recall memories of rides on the fire engine red and gold train that circled the small lake or strolling down Main Street.

Walking into this large building, fully decorated, was enough to overwhelm the senses. Just past the grand piano was a small rise where the restaurant tables were set and never a napkin out of place. Roughly another ten feet and a couple steps down revealed the entrance to "Main Street". It was hard to believe that a whole street could be found inside a building. To a small child, this street seemed endless. The candy cane decorated lampposts were only outdone by the window treatments of the shops that lined the street. Walking past each shop, peering in the windows, nothing mundane could be found. From fresh ice cream shops displaying all their flavors to a candle maker pulling and designing elegant wax, everything on Main Street seemed to be designed to enhance the joyous season.

One place which happened to be located on the PTL grounds was the adoption agency that Sonny and Fran had contacted earlier in the year. Although ineligible to adopt, Sonny found himself walking in the front door of the agency on behalf of dear friends back in New York. Having been unable to conceive, their friends were able to adopt and add two beautiful members to their family. It wouldn't be until sometime later when God, through the words of a prophet from Nigeria, would open up her womb. But that is a story for another time.

Walking into the adoption office, Sonny introduced himself. He told the woman at the front desk that he was the one who called to pick up an application. As she shuffled through the files, Sonny felt the Lord prompting him to ask one more time on behalf of himself. He quickly explained about being told previously that he and his wife were ineligible due to their age. The woman kindly apologized and said, "I'm just a volunteer and have no knowledge of the situation. However, the Assistant Director is presently in the office, I could mention it to her if you wish?"

"Thank you."

The Assistant Director met with Sonny. She introduced herself as Mary B. It was a very pleasant conversation and yet as it progressed it seemed that it was still very unlikely they would be able to adopt. Suddenly becoming aware of how much time had passed, Sonny asked if he could quickly be excused for a moment as his wife, child and granddaughter were waiting in the car. Walking back into the agency with his wife and the children, something had changed. Mary's countenance seemed positively different. When Sonny walked through the door holding the hands of his son and granddaughter on each side, Mary knew this meeting was ordained. In his right hand standing between him and his wife, was Daneal, a blond-haired fair skinned little girl and in his left, a dark eyed brown Indian boy. It was all that Mary could do to contain herself. With that, she made them promise to return the following day.

Late the next morning, Sonny and Fran returned to the adoption agency. As soon as they entered they were happily greeted by both the Assistant Director, Mary, and the present Director, Jene. There was a lot of unusual excitement in the office that day, yet up to that point, it remained a mystery as to why. During the course of their meeting, the Director and others with her, asked politely on several different occasions to be excused and each time they returned, they became more excited. Finally, they came out and said, "We know this has been a little unorthodox but we have something amazing to share with you." So, little by little, they began to piece together, for Sonny and Fran, the chain of events which led right up to that very moment.

On the morning of Monday, December 23, 1986, all the members of the adoption agency met with the birth mother to pray that God would send loving parents who would adopt her son. Someone who would help him grow in grace and in the knowledge of Jesus Christ. A family who would always love him and cherish him as their own. The mother was even more specific, in her prayers, when she beseeched God to send the adoptive family through the doors of the agency. Little did she know how quickly her prayers would be answered.

That afternoon Sonny would stop in to pick up the application for his friends. It wasn't until that moment when he walked back in with Daniel in one hand and Daneal in the other, that Mary B would recognize the answer to their prayers was now standing right in front of her. The child's mother was Irish and his birth father was East Indian. From the moment that Sonny and Fran walked in with a little Irish girl and Indian boy, there was no questioning that this was of God. Immediately after Sonny and Fran left that day, Mary B contacted Jene, the Senior Director, and could barely contain her excitement as she told her the day's events. The next day, following their meeting Jene said, "We're breaking all the rules, but we know you're sent of God."

On Saturday, December 28th Sonny and Fran left South Carolina feeling extremely elated. Unbeknownst to them, their new son, Caleb was born the very next day. Right there in the hospital, Caleb's birth mother with agency staff and friends held a little dedication service. They prayed for Caleb's protection and God's fulfilled purpose in his life. For Sonny and Fran, there was much to do in preparation of this new addition to their family. First order of business was getting an update on their home study as well as making sure all the necessary documents were in order. But God even seemed to have His divine hand in this, as everything was apparently managed without a hiccup.

February of 1987, Sonny and Fran, along with friends and family, returned to South Carolina. While there it started to snow and didn't stop. Many businesses closed early and the streets, which normally saw a fair amount of traffic, now seemed desolate. What was puzzling was, for as much as it snowed, there was little more than two inches of snow on the ground. Yet, it was enough for people to break life's routine and go home early.

Early one evening, Sonny and Fran received a call from Caleb's social worker. Their new child Caleb, who was by this time under the temporary care of another family, was extremely sick and no one was available to get him the medication he needed. They jumped in their vehicle, drove to the pharmacy to pick up the medication and delivered it to his foster parents. It was extremely unusual for adoptive parents to meet with a child for the first time without the social worker present, but due to the snow, this was exactly how events played out. As if all the moments up to this point hadn't confirmed enough that Caleb was meant to be a part of their lives, their very first look at their new child said it all.

A few days later, just before they prepared to make the long journey home, Caleb officially became a member of their family. Everyone was overwhelmed with excitement as Sonny and Fran walked through the door holding this little child. This child that was without a doubt from Jesus Himself and destined for great things. On the evening that they brought Caleb home, amongst family and friends, Caleb's life was once again dedicated to the Lord; and before the Lord, Caleb's parents, now overjoyed, praised God for their new son. For when God does something, rest assured, He does it perfectly.

ELISHA RAISES THE SHUNAMMIITE'S SON

One day Elisha went to Shunem. And a well-to-do woman was there, who urged him to stay for a meal. So whenever he came by, he stopped there to eat. She said to her husband, "I know that this man who often comes our way is a holy man of God. Let's make a small room on the roof and put in it a bed and a table, a chair and a lamp for him. Then he can stay there whenever he comes to us."

One day when Elisha came, he went up to his room and lay down there. He said to his servant Gehazi, "Call the Shunammite." So he called her, and she stood before him. Elisha said to him, "Tell her, 'You have gone to all this trouble for us. Now what can be done for you? Can we speak on your behalf to the king or the commander of the army?'"

She replied, "I have a home among my own people."

"What can be done for her?" Elisha asked.

Gehazi said, "She has no son, and her husband is old."

Then Elisha said, "Call her." So he called her, and she stood in the doorway. "About this time next year," Elisha said, "you will hold a son in your arms."

"No, my lord!" she objected. "Please, man of God, don't mislead your servant!"

But the woman became pregnant, and the next year about that same time she gave birth to a son, just as Elisha had told her.

The child grew, and one day he went out to his father, who was with the reapers. He said to his father, "My head! My head!"

His father told a servant, "Carry him to his mother." After the servant had lifted him up and carried him to his mother, the boy sat on her lap until noon, and then he died. She went up and laid him on the bed of the man of God, then shut the door and went out.

She called her husband and said, "Please send me one of the servants and a donkey so I can go to the man of God quickly and return."

"Why go to him today?" he asked. "It's not the New Moon or the Sabbath."

"That's all right," she said.

She saddled the donkey and said to her servant, "Lead on; don't slow down for me unless I tell you." So she set out and came to the man of God at Mount Carmel.

When he saw her in the distance, the man of God said to his servant Gehazi, "Look! There's the Shunammite! Run to meet her and ask her, 'Are you all right? Is your husband all right? Is your child all right?'"

"Everything is all right," she said.

When she reached the man of God at the mountain, she took hold of his feet. Gehazi came over to push her away, but the man of God said, "Leave her alone! She is in bitter distress, but the LORD has hidden it from me and has not told me why."

"Did I ask you for a son, my lord?" she said. "Didn't I tell you, 'Don't raise my hopes'?"

Elisha said to Gehazi, "Tuck your cloak into your belt, take my staff in your hand and run. Don't greet anyone you meet, and if anyone greets you, do not answer. Lay my staff on the boy's face."

But the child's mother said, "As surely as the LORD lives and as you live, I will not leave you." So he got up and followed her.

Gehazi went on ahead and laid the staff on the boy's face, but there was no sound or response. So Gehazi went back to meet Elisha and told him, "The boy has not awakened."

When Elisha reached the house, there was the boy lying dead on his couch. He went in, shut the door on the two of them and prayed to the LORD. Then he got on the bed and lay on the boy, mouth to mouth, eyes to eyes, hands to hands. As he stretched himself out on him, the boy's body grew warm. Elisha turned away and walked back and forth in the room and then got on the bed and stretched out on him once more. The boy sneezed seven times and opened his eyes.

Elisha summoned Gehazi and said, "Call the Shunammite." And he did. When she came, he said, "Take your son." She came in, fell at his feet and bowed to the ground. Then she took her son and went out.

2 Kings 4:8-37 (NIV)

☙ SPIRITED AWAY ☙

It was just past six in the morning. With daylight now peering through the beige Venetian blinds, the chances were slim that Daniel would be sleeping in this morning. Still lying in bed half asleep, he let out a big yawn, followed by rubbing the night out of his eyes. With that, this day turned ruthless.

Just a little amount of pressure was all it took for the foreign object to scrape its way across Daniel's eye as he rubbed it. The pain was immediate and intense. Never in his wildest dreams did he ever think the eye was capable of producing such unrelenting pain and discomfort. He unconsciously clenched his jaw as he struggled to look through his bathroom medicine cabinet for something to ease the pain. Now, having taken medicine, he laid back down in bed. Closing his eyes brought short minimal relief.

There was even the hope of falling back to sleep, but that was futile. To add insult to injury, whatever it was that caused the abrasion could still be felt moving around in his eye.

Two hours had passed and after failing to fall asleep, let alone get any relief, Daniel found that the worst of the pain was yet to come. It felt as if a nail was being driven into his eye. The throbbing he felt behind his bloodshot eye nearly brought him to tears, but he struggled to hold them back as the tears made the stinging more intense. The migraine of all migraines followed leaving him extremely nauseous, dizzy, now exhausted and in a whole lot of pain. Barely able to move, he tried praying to God to relieve this pain from his eye and head. But when immediate healing seemed out of the cards, he prayed that God would just give him a moment of relief. Unable to even get out of bed, he reached over to his phone and called his parents, who were just downstairs, and asked them to pray and bring him something for his head. Nothing seemed to help; that's when he thought this may be something more serious.

The room felt warmer than usual, who would have thought you could run a fever from getting scratched in the eye. He couldn't turn on the ceiling fan in an effort to keep cooler, because the wind exasperated the pain. Struggling through the searing pain, with one eye, he navigated through his phone. He search various articles about corneal abrasions and eye damage. It only took reading a handful of articles, which included phrases such as: permanent damage, infection, loss of vision, and seek medical attention immediately, to have Daniel calling for an emergency appointment with his optometrist.

The drive to the optometrist was complete horror. It wasn't long into the ride that Daniel realized he should have taken his parents up on their offer to drive him. With his damaged eye more than ¾ closed and rapidly blinking, he struggled to maintain focused on the road. To make matters worse, the migraine had intensified. Daniel found himself squinting his other eye as well. Up until this time, the pain had been so horrific that Daniel never had a chance to assess how something had entered his eye.

He didn't have to sit long in the optometrist's office. However, because of this splitting headache, Daniel did what he could to keep from focusing on the pounding in his head. The florescent bulbs recessed above seemed to be brighter than usual. With elbows resting on his knees and head resting in the palms of his hands, Daniel gently closed his eyes. There in the waiting room, for the first time he found himself starting to drift off to sleep when the doctor came in and said, "Daniel, we're ready for you."

From the moment Dr. T.H. saw Daniel's bloodshot eye, he knew he had to be in a lot of discomfort. Dr. T.H. was very thorough in examining his eye and the surrounding area. Various instruments and lenses were used to examine the eye before he ultimately placed the dye drops in. There must have been a little bit of a numbing characteristic to those drops, because for the first time Daniel could feel the pain subsiding. Once the drops were in, the doctor moved his lens in place. The dye made visible the long scratch running from one side to almost the other side of Daniel's eye, just below his pupil. The Doctor said, "Well, you have a pretty good-sized scrape running along your eye. Do you know how it could have possibly happened?"

Daniel described all the events from that morning but still couldn't identify what or how anything could have made its way into his eye. Feeling as if the object was still in his eye, Daniel asked Dr. T.H. for the second time, to look to see if any foreign object could be found. He looked under each eyelid, as well as thoroughly examined every part of the eye possible. He explained that during a corneal abrasion, until healed, it will feel as something is still in the eye. The Doctor wrote him a prescription for an antibiotic and told him to make a follow-up appointment. Although still in pain, Daniel left the office feeling a little more at ease. By this time the headache was more a nuisance than the eye. After leaving the office, Daniel immediately went to the pharmacy to have his prescription filled. It would take roughly an hour. So, Daniel decided rather than wait, he would take a ride back to the pharmacy once they called to say it was ready.

When he arrived home, Daniel's parents immediately asked how the office visit went. He quickly told them all the details followed by telling them, due to his awful headache, he needed to go lay down. Knowing Daniel needed to run back out to get his prescription, his father drove to the pharmacy once they called to say it was ready. It was a pleasant surprise for Daniel to see his prescription already sitting there on the kitchen island, sparing him the ride to pick it up.

The next morning when he awoke, he was extremely grateful to find the headache was completely gone. He caught himself a few times unconsciously making a move to rub his eyes, but always managed to stop himself before he did. Daniel was pretty religious about taking his drops on time. After reading all those articles about the worst-case scenarios, he knew God only gave him two eyes and he wasn't going to take them for granted. Despite knowing that one of the characteristics of a corneal abrasion is to feel like an object is still in one's eye, he was almost certain something was still there. He constantly found himself checking in the mirror but never could spot anything. *Perhaps the doctor was right. Maybe there was nothing there anymore. Maybe it's just a symptom of the scratch.* He was ready to resign the feeling of the foreign object in his eye to what the doctor told him when he felt that foreign sensation in a different part of his eye. Undoubtedly there was something there, but what was it?

That night as Daniel made another attempt to wash the foreign body from his eye, he noticed a face scrub that he had been using the last few days. It was as if a light bulb went on above his head. What had scratched his eye just the morning before was one of the small sand-like scrubbing components in the facial scrub. After ten-minutes of flushing his eye out with over-the-counter rinses, Daniel was sure that whatever was in there, wasn't there anymore. Daniel went to bed feeling somewhat elated that finally the foreign object was free from his eye.

The following morning felt like the first in forever where he didn't have the annoying burden of a foreign object dancing around under his eyelids, waiting for another opportunity to wreak havoc on his eye. After two days of being nearly incapacitated it was nice to finally be able to get something done, and today was about getting some of the overdue yard work accomplished. No sooner did he walk out his garage door, did that pesky feeling of something in his eye return. Once again he went inside and in front of his bathroom mirror he flushed and searched his eye. He wasn't sure if he was able to remove it, but at least he couldn't feel it anymore. Maybe he finally got it? Daniel went back outside and proceeded to trim some of the greenery in the front yard. It wasn't too long before he felt something in his eye once again. Daniel was completely disheartened. On the verge of tears, in one last desperate attempt to find some relief, he asked God to miraculously take this object from his eye. But would He answer?

Standing alone on his uncut lawn, the moment suddenly seemed different. It was extremely peaceful and familiar. The nostalgic feeling of when he was seven years old, laying on his front lawn staring at the sky, watching the clouds pass by as he listened to the breeze sing through the trees. Looking around he noticed all was quiet and abnormally still. There were no birds chirping, no sound of the neighbor's lawnmower, or even the murmuring of the wind. The palms which normally whispered in the breeze seemed to be frozen in place as if time stood still for a moment. Then without warning cutting through the still quietness came a strong cool breeze. Daniel watched the path in the grass as the wind raced towards him. The trees now elegantly swayed as the wind blew through the palms. The breeze wasn't incredibly strong but Daniel was still surprised as he underestimated its strength once it hit him. Almost as quickly as it had arrived, it was gone. Daniel stood there as the cool breeze raced past him, wisped from his eye that foreign object and with it all stinging sensations. With a smile and eyes tearing, Daniel thanked his Savior for caring so much that He took the time to answer his request. Through this miracle, God affirmed that He is our ever present help, even in our smallest matters.

Are not five sparrows sold for two pennies? Yet not one of them is forgotten by God. Indeed, the very hairs of your head are all numbered. Don't be afraid; you are worth more than many sparrows. Luke 12:6-7 (NIV)

A BLIND BEGGAR RECEIVES HIS SIGHT

As Jesus approached Jericho, a blind man was sitting by the roadside begging. When he heard the crowd going by, he asked what was happening. They told him, "Jesus of Nazareth is passing by."

He called out, "Jesus, Son of David, have mercy on me!"

Those who led the way rebuked him and told him to be quiet, but he shouted all the more, "Son of David, have mercy on me!"

Jesus stopped and ordered the man to be brought to him. When he came near, Jesus asked him, "What do you want me to do for you?"

"Lord, I want to see," he replied.

Jesus said to him, "Receive your sight; your faith has healed you." Immediately he received his sight and followed Jesus, praising God. When all the people saw it, they also praised God.

Luke 18:35-43 (NIV)

◎ ANGELS ON THE L.I.E ◎

It was a little after eight in the morning and Sonny was taking his usual commute into the city. It was quite a long trip to have to travel every morning, but he was more than willing to do what was needed to provide for his family. There was no lack of traffic westbound on the Long Island Expressway, but it was moving surprisingly well. It was never a thought when he woke up that morning, that he would have yet another story to add to the many times in his life when God protected him from certain death.

His commute gave him time to pray for the day and begin to organize in his mind the work that needed to be accomplished. A few years back, God opened up an amazing opportunity for Sonny to go into business for himself; and to this day, God has used that business to provide, not only for him and his family, but many others as well. The story about how God directed Sonny into this business and the act of faith that was required is an amazing one, but meant for another time.

Westbound traffic on the L.I.E. was moving nicely. A steady 70 mph, so there was little need to do the usual weaving in and out of traffic. The forecast called for possible rain, but during his commute the sun broke through the clouds and brightened the morning sky. Sonny could feel the warmth from the sun's rays as they breached the back window of his car and landed on his right arm which sat atop the armrest. Comfortable in the far left lane, Sonny was making amazing time. -Anyone who has any experience with driving on the L.I.E. knows traffic can be a daunting task, especially during the morning rush.- It seemed all signs pointed toward this turning out to be a good day.

What was this woman in a red minivan, oblivious to all others around her, thinking? Sonny looked out his right window to find her riding alongside him; sometimes inching too close but there wasn't anywhere he could go, as there was a car behind him and another in front. Then she quickly started to merge into his lane, evidently unaware he was alongside her. By this time traffic was heavier but still moving very nicely. Without regard, she turned her wheel. Swiftly reacting, Sonny jerked his steering wheel to the left to avoid getting sideswiped but now found himself in an even more precarious situation. Now fast approaching was the concrete median that separated the eastbound and westbound traffic. Sonny once again turned his steering wheel, but this time to avoid the concrete barrier. During this evasive maneuver, he lost control of his car and shot across three lanes of very dense traffic where he found himself facing eastbound on the right shoulder.

Sitting there with his hands still on the wheel, he let out a big sigh. As he took a few moments to decompress, he looked at the traffic as it passed him and knew what had just happened was absolutely impossible. He knew beyond a shadow of a doubt that God had sent angels to clear a path through this traffic and had He not, Sonny would most likely not be alive to share this story.

JESUS CALMS THE STORM

One day Jesus said to his disciples, "Let us go over to the other side of the lake." So they got into a boat and set out. As they sailed, He fell asleep. A squall came down on the lake, so that the boat was being swamped, and they were in great danger.

The disciples went and woke him, saying, "Master, Master, we're going to drown!"

He got up and rebuked the wind and the raging waters; the storm subsided, and all was calm. "Where is your faith?" he asked his disciples.

In fear and amazement they asked one another, "Who is this? He commands even the winds and the water, and they obey him."

Luke 8:22-25 (NIV)

ꝏ $5 ꝏ

It was a crisp green five-dollar bill. It looked brand new. Not like the dollars that her mom had in her pocketbook. She noticed the man on the front. She had seen him before, but where? Oh yeah that's right. He is the guy that's embossed on all the stray pennies she collected on top of her dresser. This wasn't just money, this was a five-dollar bill that she earned for helping her mom with chores. Rachel, only four years old, loved following her mother around the house, helping out where she could. So, when her mom pulled out a crisp five-dollar bill from a bank envelope and handed it to her, Rachel's eyes widened as she thought of all the things this money could buy her. She often saw her mother paying for things at the store, but noticed she rarely used coins. It was always a card or little green pieces of paper with men on the front, and now she had one.

What would she buy? A brand new stuffed animal, perhaps a doll, maybe a pink bike like the one she saw on TV. Why not a pony? That night, as she fell asleep, she couldn't help but think of all the things she could buy with her money tomorrow, as her mother promised to take her shopping after the morning's church service.

Finally falling asleep, her mother took the money, which had fallen from her small hand onto the bed, and placed it on top of the dresser. She kissed her forehead, prayed for her and whispered "goodnight".

The following morning when Rachel awoke, she immediately noticed the money was missing from her hand. She frantically pulled up the sheets looking everywhere on the bed, before she finally noticed it on the dresser. It was going to be an exciting day because after church, her mother and she were going to have a girls' day out. Rachel got herself dressed, slipped her money into her sparkly pink purse and waited patiently while her mother got ready for church. She couldn't help continually opening up her little purse to check that her five-dollar bill was still there. Yep, there it was, right where she put it.

Church seemed longer today, but that was because Rachel couldn't wait until it was over. One thing that did catch her eye was when people started passing a silver plate around. She watched the plate move from one aisle to the next as people placed money in it. She tapped her mom and asked, "Why are they putting dollars in there?"

Her mother responded, "That money goes to people who need help."

Clearly evident from the look on her face, Rachel pondered her mother's response as she looked down at her crisp five-dollar bill.

With the word *Amen* the pastor ended the service. Immediately, a big smile came over Rachel's face as she looked up at her mother who asked, "Are you ready, Rachel?" With a big nod she gave her answer. Looking at Rachel in her little car seat through the rearview mirror, her mother couldn't help but smile at the steadfast grin that ornamented Rachel's face as she kicked her little feet to the rhythm of the car radio.

Pulling into the store parking lot, Rachel knew it was almost time to get the toy of her dreams. She envisioned endless aisles of toys all for the picking and all available now that she had her own money. Walking up to the automatic doors, a poor old man stood hunched over with a sign. Rachel wasn't able to read all that well yet, so she asked her mother what it said. The sign read: "In need of help, food or money, God bless." From the looks of his clothing and the tone of his voice, as he thanked the few people who bothered to stop and give, he seemed genuine in his request for help. Rachel pulled from her sparkly pink purse her five-dollar bill and handed it to the man. His eyes welled up as he gently took the money from her hand and thanked her. Rachel's mother looked on as she struggled to hold back tears herself. Rachel looked up at her mother and smiled, then they proceeded into the store. Once beyond the entrance, Rachel's mother told her that she'd done a good thing and Jesus would bless her. Of all the toys she looked at, the one that caught her eye was one of the little trinkets on the checkout aisle. So, to reward her previous kindness, her mother bought her this in addition to a bag of candy. Now back in the car, Rachel's mother asked, "Where would you like to go for lunch?" already knowing what the answer would be.

They pulled up to the fast food restaurant and went inside. Rachel already knew what she was getting and best of all it came with the greatest toy. Chicken nuggets, fries and an amazing toy. What could be better? Rachel looked up, unable to see over the counter, as her mother ordered the food. Suddenly feeling a tap on her shoulder, Rachel's mother turned around to be greeted by an older lady with a nice smile. She said, "You have such a beautiful daughter. Please allow me to be a blessing and pay for your lunch today."

Initially, her mother's response was, "We really appreciate that but it's ok."

The lady insisted. Liz knew that this was God returning her daughter's earlier generosity. Now sitting across the small square table, Rachel's mother explained to her that because of her kindness to the man earlier, God blessed them both with a meal. With a smile Rachel responded, "And a toy."

THE WEDDING AT CANA

On the third day a wedding took place at Cana in Galilee. Jesus' mother was there, and Jesus and his disciples had also been invited to the wedding. When the wine was gone, Jesus' mother said to him, "They have no more wine."

"Woman, why do you involve me?" Jesus replied. "My hour has not yet come."

His mother said to the servants, "Do whatever he tells you."

Nearby stood six stone water jars, the kind used by the Jews for ceremonial washing, each holding from twenty to thirty gallons.

Jesus said to the servants, "Fill the jars with water"; so they filled them to the brim.

Then he told them, "Now draw some out and take it to the master of the banquet."

They did so, and the master of the banquet tasted the water that had been turned into wine. He did not realize where it had come from, though the servants who had drawn the water knew. Then he called the bridegroom aside and said, "Everyone brings out the choice wine first and then the cheaper wine after the guests have had too much to drink; but you have saved the best till now."

What Jesus did here in Cana of Galilee was the first of the signs through which he revealed his glory; and his disciples believed in him.

John 2:1-11 (NIV)

ⓠ THE BOOK ⓠ

Daniel opened his eyes and noticed that he was standing. The place was so unimaginably bright that he wondered how he wasn't blind. Peering through his squinted eyes he noticed something was different about this light. This all-encompassing light didn't radiate the yellowish hue normally seen in sunlight. He heard the faint sound of music in the distance. It sounded like many different songs being played and sung, yet somehow were able to harmonize. As his eyes slowly continued to adjust, he noticed to his right and left, roughly fifty-feet from where he stood, were columns of fire. No amount of squinting at this point could sharpen his vision, but what he could see was that these columns started at what appeared to be the ground and rose roughly twenty feet. At the top of these columns, flames didn't shoot away much like expected from the nature of fire. Rather, they seemed to be cut off, as if someone were able to cut straight across the fire like scissors to a piece of paper. Looking down he noticed even his feet were lost in this radiant white light which also reflected off the ground. As his eyes continued to adjust, he faintly began to notice other objects in the area. But something else was odd. There was not a shadow to be seen. This light, so overwhelming, seemed to run similar to water, creeping into the smallest of places giving darkness no chance to hide.

Daniel wasn't afraid or apprehensive. In fact, there was a peace unlike anything he had ever felt before. There were no thoughts of how he had come to this place. No immediate thoughts of family or friends and what they could be doing. The only reality was here in this moment. This interminable moment where time stretched into eternity with the second hand on this clock never to tick again. He noticed a slight tingle to the tops of his hands. Viewing his hands then his arms, he noticed that familiar beauty mark on the inside of his right arm and yet something strangely different. His skin appeared new. The scars from that childhood bike accident on his hands were now gone and the mark left as a reminder of when he nearly cut his finger off, was nowhere to be found.

With eyes now better adjusted to the light, he looked forward and noticed a big altar. This altar was made of some unknown wood. Judging by the extreme detail, it had to be made by a craftsman with a masterful hand unlike any other.

Even from the thirty-five foot distance that he stood, Daniel noticed the amount of precision it must have taken. Inside the beveled edged and engraved lines was gold. As if it was freshly fired molten and poured, this liquid gold flowed freely through the beveled and engraved lines reflecting that same white light which was commonplace. On this finely crafted altar sat a big book. It was brownish and from the looks of it, very old. If there was an illogical way to describe this book, it would be that the book looked new but at the same time old and like everything else, this book radiated that all-encompassing light.

This light seemed to originate from some distance behind the altar. Daniel, his eyes now nearly fully adjusted, still found it somewhat uncomfortable to focus his sight directly forward. The light became exponentially brighter as it moved closer to the altar. Daniel turned his head away for a moment to give his eyes rest and noticed those fiery pillars once again.

For some time now, Daniel had a pretty good idea of where he was. Yet, it wasn't until that moment when he looked away that he was certain. He was completely amazed to see those fiery columns that he noticed earlier, were in fact fiery swords. With complete dedication these huge angelic beings stood upright. With sword handle tightly gripped in their right hand, sword parallel to their bodies and the tip touching the ground, they stood firmly at attention. Now able to see, he also noticed there was an angel standing in procession every ten feet. Briefly turning and looking over his right shoulder he discovered the procession of angels stretched as far as he could see.

A thunderous sound came from the light behind the altar. Daniel focused his attention ahead of him. The light seemed to be much brighter, perhaps because it now was closer to the altar. Still a little difficult to see, he noticed inside this radiant light was the silhouette of a man. He tried to squint to get a better look but the light was too bright. At once a hand appeared from this light. It was a big rough hand, like a farmer's, carpenter's or another working with his hands. The hand itself emanated this light as well. While this hand reached to open the book, Daniel noticed the scar that adorned its wrist. With a gentle touch He opened the cover. With that, a rushing wind came and began to flip the pages.

Much like the book, the pages looked aged but at the same time appeared to be made of the finest paper possible. Rapidly page after page turned. It completely defied all logic the amount of pages that continued to turn for the size of the book. As he continued to observe, Daniel's mind digressed to another time.

@

Daniel, no more than seven years old, peeked carefully out from underneath his covers to find these green goblin like creatures dancing around his red and white car bed. He desperately wanted to call for his mom and dad but kept silent as to not make aware his presence to these little creatures. Then one of the dancing beings stopped and noticed Daniel's one eye peering out. Daniel's little heart jumped into the pit of his stomach as he pulled the blanket down and closed his eyes. Then everything went silent. Hoping they were now gone, Daniel carefully peeked out again from underneath the slightly lifted corner of his blanket, only to notice inches from his face was a creature staring back at him. Daniel screamed as loud as he could. Shaking Daniel's shoulder at 1:30 a.m., his mother and father gently woke him up from this nightmare. They tried to reassure him that this was just a dream, but it appeared there was little chance they were getting back to sleep anytime soon.

Daniel's screaming also awoke his younger brother Caleb, who was laying in the bed on the other side of the room. It seemed it was going to be another long night for both parents, however it only took a few minutes of Caleb's father rocking him, before he fell back to sleep. He gently placed Caleb back into his bed, at which time he was told, by his wife, to go back to bed and that she would wait until Daniel fell back to sleep. Daniel's mother told him to think of the most amazing place you can, and imagine you're there.

Daniel responded, "I'm going to think of heaven."

"That's a perfect place," she said.

Then she began to sing.

Normally it was like clockwork. By the end of her third song all the children would be asleep. But tonight, following this dream, Daniel couldn't be more awake. She could tell from the look on her son's face that he was lost in thought and no sooner did she finish her singing did he ask, "Is heaven really real?"

She responded, "Yes, it is. It's a wonderful place with no more sadness, no more pain, and no more nightmares. A place where everything is perfect. Even the lion and the lamb will be friends."

Then Daniel asked, "If I'm really good can I go?"

She replied, "Being good enough will not get you into heaven. Believing in Jesus is the only way to wipe all our sins clean and be allowed into heaven."

He interrupted, "What is a sin?"

"A sin is anytime you do or say something wrong."

She continued by saying, "Even if you sinned once in your whole life, you still would not be allowed into heaven because heaven is a place of perfection and God cannot allow sin to enter. When Jesus came to earth, He lived a perfect life without sin and when He died on the cross, He took upon Himself all mankind's sin. See, it's an act of faith not works."

He replied, "What do you mean?"

She tried to figure out the best way to make this understandable for her seven year old son and responded, "God made getting into heaven very easy. There is nothing you have to do or can do to get into heaven. You need to just believe in the Lord Jesus Christ. When He died, took your sins and rose again on the third day, He was presented as a living atonement for all of your sins. Now when God sees you, He sees you as if you never sinned because Jesus took your sins. And now you can enter heaven."

He asked, "So what do I do?"

She responded, "Simply believe and repeat this prayer after me:

"Dear Lord Jesus. I love You. Please forgive my sins. I believe You died on a cross for my sins and rose again. Please come into my heart so that I can live with You forever. Amen."

She looked him directly in his eyes and said, "Daniel, at this very moment all the angels in heaven are rejoicing because your name is now written in the Lamb's book of life."

"What is that?" he asked.

"It is a very important book which contains the names of all those who believe in the Lord Jesus Christ. All the names of those who are allowed to enter heaven, and now your name can be found in it."

@

The rushing sound of the wind intensified to an almost deafening roar. Daniel watched as the turning pages began to accelerate. He looked around for any signs of wind that would produce such a sound but could not even find the hem of the angel's garments in motion. As if the light reflecting off everything wasn't intense enough, the liquid fiery gold substance in the altar and the fire in the angels' swords seemed to radiate brighter than before. In fact, everything now seemed more radiant. The faint sound of the music afar seemed clearer. He couldn't understand how he was able to hear the music clearer now with this rushing sound of wind. Perhaps the music was traveling on this wind? Is that even possible? Then again is this place even possible? Logical? Absolutely not.

Daniel, for the first time, was able to notice that he was in what appeared to be an enormous hall. Unsure of how he knew the exact height, he could now see the amazing arches which graced the thousand-meter high ceiling which had an element that seemed to mimic the sight of shimmering finely broken glass reflecting in the sunlight. The hall must have been as long as it was tall because when he turned to look back he couldn't see an end. Any attempt to make out objects beyond the altar was futile with the radiant light bleaching out all space behind it.

The abrupt halt to the roaring sound caused Daniel to once again focus his attention ahead of him. How long have these pages been turning? It could have been hours or minutes. There was no sense of time and nothing to measure it by. Turning his head for a brief moment, he noticed the angels now held their swords extended with the tip of their blades now pointing towards the center of the ceiling. Everything became extremely tranquil as the wind pushed over one last page. Moments later, Daniel regained sight of the hand which came out of that intense light hovering above the book and heard a voice saying, "Come and look." It was a strong thunderous voice, but at the same time gentle and filled with love. With each step forward Daniel had no words to describe what he was feeling. It was a flood of emotions with every step and behind him a trail of tears marked his path. Now standing just off to the side of the altar, the hand pointed towards a page in the book. Daniel turned and looked at the elegant page which had but one name on it. It was his!

Upon catching closer sight of the wound on His wrist, Daniel fell to the floor and with his head down began to cry. Tears of joy, pain, heartache, shame, and regret all seemed to merge into one emotion. Whether because the intensity of the light had pacified or because Daniel's eyes were now completely adjusted, he now could see the feet and robe of the man that stood before him emanating light. With his head still bowed Daniel caught sight between his blinding tears of the wounds in the sides of this man's heels. Daniel reached out to touch the wounds but pulled his hands back and cried, "Thank you Savior, for taking these wounds for me." Daniel still dared not look up. All he could see was the slight reflection through the puddle of tears which drenched the floor in front of him. Jesus knelt down slowly and placed each hand under the sides of Daniel's face and directed his face upward. From the moment Jesus touched his face, Daniel could feel nothing but love. This love was beyond description, unlike anything even thought possible. Those tears which ran because of so many emotions before, now ran because of this indescribable love. With that, Jesus placed both of His thumbs in the corners of Daniel's eyes and pushed them outward wiping the tears from his face. Daniel momentarily regained sight of the wounds in His wrists and once again became overwhelmed with emotion. But this time, no tears ran. Daniel looked up and for the first time beheld the eyes of his Savior. Gazing into His eyes; eternity past, present, and future were instantly made known. The color was unlike anything that could be described and the love seen in His eyes was enough to cover the world infinite times over. Daniel had waited his whole life for this moment and now that moment was here. The Lord smiled and said, "Well done my good and faithful servant, join Me in paradise."

THE PROMISE

If you declare with your mouth, "Jesus is Lord," and believe in your heart that God raised him from the dead, you will be saved. For it is with your heart that you believe and are justified, and it is with your mouth that you profess your faith and are saved.

Romans 10: 9-10 (NIV)

For God so loved the world that he gave his one and only Son, that whoever believes in him shall not perish but have eternal life. For God did not send his Son into the world to condemn the world, but to save the world through him. Whoever believes in him is not condemned, but whoever does not believe stands condemned already because they have not believed in the name of God's one and only Son.

John 3:16-18 (NIV)

On the first day of the week, very early in the morning, the women took the spices they had prepared and went to the tomb. They found the stone rolled away from the tomb, but when they entered, they did not find the body of the Lord Jesus. While they were wondering about this, suddenly two men in clothes that gleamed like lightning stood beside them. In their fright the women bowed down with their faces to the ground, but the men said to them, "Why do you look for the living among the dead? He is not here; he has risen!

Remember how he told you, while he was still with you in Galilee: The Son of Man must be delivered over to the hands of sinners, be crucified and on the third day be raised again." Then they remembered his words.

Luke 24:1-8 (NIV)

"Let not your heart be troubled; you believe in God, believe also in Me. In My Father's house are many mansion if it were not so, I would have told you. I go to prepare a place for you. And if I go and prepare a place for you, I will come again and receive you to Myself; that where I am, there you may be also. And where I go you know, and the way you know."

Thomas said to Him, "Lord, we do not know where You are going, and how can we know the way?"

Jesus said to him, "I am the way, the truth, and the life. No one comes to the Father except through Me.

John 14:1-6 (NKJV)

ⓠ THE END IS JUST THE BEGINNING ⓠ

This book has been an extremely enlightening experience and over the course of writing it, God was as much speaking to me as any other. I, as much as anyone, fell into the mindset of fully believing God was the God of the miraculous. That the *Dunamis* power of God was there, but it was always for someone else somewhere else. While researching for this book, God showed me just how much He has intervened in my life and the lives of those dearest to me. Writing these stories has been a faith building experience and clearly it was something not meant for me to keep to myself.

It is my sincerest prayer that God has used the stories in this book to build your faith or perhaps, even renew a faith forgotten. One of the most important things that God has taught me over the last year is the value He places on a human soul. So, if this book through the divine hand of God is able to uplift, restore and perhaps bring about a true relationship with Jesus Christ, if all the effort, time and resources spent on it was for but one person, it has been well worth it.

When God miraculously intervenes on our behalf it can happen in any number of ways. In fact, that number is infinite. But the main purpose it serves is threefold. The first is to give glory to our Heavenly Father. The second is to serve as a reminder that God loves you and is forever taking an active role in your life; building your faith and strengthening the relationship you have with your Lord. Lastly, it serves as a testimony to others. A story of God's faithfulness and love in your life and how He is waiting to do the same for them.

I really do hope that God has used the stories in this book to help restore your faith in, or affirm to you that God is still in the business of performing miraculous works today. In the same way the testimonies in this book may have affected you, I ask you now to do the same for another.

Following this chapter you will find many blank pages. I ask you to please finish this book for me by writing down your own testimony. A truly divine moment when God acted in His *Dunamis* power on your behalf. It can be a testimony of healing, provision, protection, sustenance, or perhaps the best miracle of all: the day you accepted Christ into your life. Once complete, please give this book to someone else. Someone who can be positively affected by this book. A book which now holds your own testimony. And remember,

> *"God can only bless what you do, not your intentions."*
>
> *Pastor Michael Bryant*

☙ YOUR TESTIMONY ☙

JEREMIAH 29:11

For I know the plans I have for you," declares the Lord, "plans to prosper you and not to harm you, plans to give you hope and a future.